"If I could use two words  ."
This guy has lived life full is
authentic, edgy, and ofter n
the hardest of hearts. John .lt
Light City Tour in the prisons of Florida just a couple of years ago. His live
presentation literally captivated every room we ministered in. We gave away
cases of his book, *Shackled,* during this tour until the inventory was depleted.
The inmates were so eager to read about a man, not unlike themselves, who had
been in their shoes and could compassionately lead them to a place of hope,
healing, and redemption."

Mark Mason—Founder and President, Life on
the Verge Ministries, Richmond, Virginia

"John Swanger's story is riveting and absolutely amazing. His first book was
just the warmup to this dramatic sequel. A must read for anyone who doubts
the possibilities of genuine, amazing transformation through Jesus, and a won-
derfully encouraging read for everyone else!"

Craig L. Blomberg—Prolific Author amd Distinguished
Professor of New Testament, Denver Seminary

"Swanger's first book, *Shackled: Confessions of a Teenage Bank Robber,* gives you
the inside look and feel of the life of a criminal, and as well an up-close view of
prison life. It is riveting and leaves you wanting more. His new book, *Unshackled: A Story of Redemption,* gives the incarcerated hope that there is life after
prison. John has ministered alongside our ministry, M.I.A., in several prisons
within the Texas prison system, and his ministry has changed the hearts and
lives of many.

Rev. Rick J. Glover—Founder and President,
M.I.A. Ministries, Lancaster, Texas

Shackled in the penitentiary of his mind is where John Swanger lived. Shackled
to betrayals and oppression at a very young age. Shackled in Lompoc Federal
Prison is where John resided by the age of 19. With anticipation, you will read
how he overcame the obstacles and challenges that defined his life. Swanger's
first book, *Shackled: Confessions of a Teenage Bank Robber,* has impacted my
16-year old son's incarcerated life in ways none other have. Through John's
honest account of life, many lives are touched. To inmates young and old,
Hope and Freedom become tangible, and a new depth and meaning to their
life are discovered. They are becoming unshackled!"

Laurie Marie Hansen

"I met John in 2011, when he came to give his testimony in Limon Correctional Facility, part of the Colorado Department of Corrections. Since then, I have ministered with John in four state prisons, and he has helped us reshape how we looked at prison ministry. It's really exciting to spend two hours, one way, on our way to a prison visit hearing stories of John's first 25 years, his amazing redemption, and dramatic accounts of his ministry to street people and we were the first ministry he was able to join behind the walls. (By the way, John has also been a phenomenal Santa with a very unique gift in the way he ministers to children and their parents!)

John Shager—Ministry Leader, Pardoned by
Christ and Authentic Manhood, Denver;
Santa Clause and Company, Denver, Colorado

John Swanger's first book, *Shackled: Confessions of a Teenage Bank Robber,* is a riveting read. He winds up in a federal prison. I think that's why the inmates he chats with now listen to John. He's been there, done that. The stories coming out of John's speaking gigs in prisons are often best told by the guards who have never seen their inmates react so favorably and enthusiastically by someone just talking to them. John's that good of a storyteller (and it's all true). This sequel, *Unshackled: A Story of Redemption*, tells the rest of the story. Buckle your seatbelts; this book completes the thrilling ride.

Mike Sares—Pastor, Scum of the Earth Church; Author, *Pure
Scum: The Left-Out, the Right-Brained, and the Grace of God*

I have had the privilege of doing youth ministry with John and Raylene Swanger for the past few years. They are a dynamic duo engaging youth in Remann Hall, Echo Glen, Naselle, and Pierce County Jail in Washington State. What I love most about them is their authenticity. They are real, and God has given them a supernatural ability to love every kid they reach out to. John's first book, *Shackled: Confessions of a Teenage Bank Robber* has been a powerful tool to connect with the kids. John's story speaks to them and it opens up opportunity for conversation and relationship. Youth ministry is the Swangers' life, not just something they do. They are all in, which is evident by the sacrifices they make. They give their books away freely in order to bring lost kids the hope and love of Jesus Christ. I am waiting in great anticipation to see how God will continue to work through John and Raylene and John's new book, *Unshackled: A Story of Redemption,* to change people's lives.

Brenda Boback—Director of Juvenile Justice Ministry,
Tacoma Area Youth For Christ, Tacoma, Washington

UNSHACKLED

A STORY OF REDEMPTION

JOHN SWANGER

Unshackled: A Story of Redemption
First Edition
Copyright © 2018 by John Swanger

To order additional books:
www.amazon.com
john@swanger.net

ISBN: 978-1-9798-8161-6
E-book also available

Book Editorial and Production: Inspira Literary Solutions, Gig Harbor, WA
Typesetting: PerfecType, Nashville, TN
Cover Design: John Swanger

Printed in the U.S.A.

THE CONTINUATION OF
A TRUE STORY

DEDICATION

Maxine Helen Jones

November 13, 1939–November 1, 2008

Maxine began her journey for the Lord back in October, 1977, when God woke her up in the middle of the night. God said, *"Maxine I want you to go find My Son, Jesus, and get baptized in His name. I have a job I want you to do."*

Maxine was the catalyst that helped launch many ministries, including our own, Cross & Clef Ministries. Maxine passed away November 1, 2008, and she is missed.

"Maxine was closer to God than anyone I have ever known. She was so close that when she died, she probably didn't notice much of a difference."

Roger Jensen

Roger, by being obedient to God, helped launch our ministry to the homeless. God told Roger to take me into his recording studio and produce an album of my songs. But Roger went above and beyond. He provided the studio, supplies, and musicians, and he let me stay in his house on my many trips to Seattle for the recording sessions. This recording launched our ministry to the poor, and I am forever grateful to him.

Raylene Swanger

From the day we met, I knew I was forever blessed to be matched with the most compassionate and loving person I had ever known. While she tells people it took her a year to start loving me, I will tell you that her love is a treasure.

Nowhere else could I ever find someone who would walk away from everything we had built and step into another life simply because God told us to. Forsaking it all for the sake of the call. And she has done it many times.

I couldn't possibly imagine a life without her. Throughout all of God's amazing creation, I simply have to look across the table to see His greatest work. Thank you, God.

FOREWORD

John Swanger's writing is unconventional; John is unconventional. John's writing is authentic; John is authentic. John's writing is raw; John is raw. John's writing is radical; John is radical. And those are all characteristics I love about John Swanger.

He is a man who is sold out to GOD and lives to share Jesus—and the miracles Jesus has done for him—with as many people as possible. John does not write one thing and live differently. What you see with him is what you get; he is simple in that way.

You are not around John long before it becomes evident that he lives to obey Jesus and do it with abandon. John's books are not mere prose; they depict the radical transformations of his life, his heart, and his actions that continue to this day.

John and his wife, Raylene, have been a part of our church family for several years, and I have had the remarkable privilege to minister with John to inmates. Unquestionably, God's hand is on him. I've watched inmates respond not just to John's story, but to him as a person because he is unconventional, authentic, raw, and radical. While he has a tough exterior, he is an extremely gentle and loving man who captures the attention and hearts of those he encounters.

Shackled (John's first book) and *Unshackled* are two page-turner books I couldn't read fast enough, eager to find out what happened next. Get ready to be challenged and blessed by *Unshackled*—and for a sleep-deprived night or two; you will find it difficult to put this book down!

Mike Riches
Lead Pastor, Harborview Fellowship, Gig Harbor, Washington
Founder and Director, The Sycamore Commission
www.sycamorecommission.org

AUTHOR'S NOTE

It feels like home. It feels like everything Raylene and I have done over the years has prepared us and led us to be right where we are now. We feel like this is what God created us to do.

To date, we have given away nearly a thousand copies of my first book, *Shackled: Confessions of a Teenage Bank Robber,* to prisoners—both adults and juveniles. We will continue to do so, and we hope to surpass that total with copies of this book: *Unshackled: A Story of Redemption.*

The book you hold in your hands is the rest of the story . . .

John Swanger
May, 2018

PROLOGUE

It was just past noon when Nash and I headed to the yard. Everyone started cheering as we walked onto the grass, and it took a minute before we realized what was happening. Someone was escaping right over the fences near the corner of the main yard. As soon as we weaved our way through the crowd we could see it was Demerol and Kentucky.

Gunfire erupted from both of the gun towers. Kentucky was shot as he headed down the inside of the first fence. He fell onto the Constantine wire but quickly rolled to the second fence and began climbing. Half way up, he took another bullet and fell back. Demerol made it over both fences and across the road. But as he was nearing the tree line he got hit in the head. He dropped like a dumbbell in the bone yard.

"Damn it!" Nash called out.

"Shit," I followed.

It was quite a contrast to how our day had begun.

Over breakfast Nash had said "The weather report is calling for heavy fog this evening." Fog was called "parole dust" because it made it difficult for the gun towers to see, thereby making the chances of a successful escape more probable. We summoned Demerol over to our table and let him know tonight was a go.

A couple of weeks earlier, Demerol, Nash, Kentucky, and I had paid an inmate in the welding department thirty dollars green to build us a bar breaker—a three-quarter-inch thick slab of steel about six inches square with a notch cut into one side and a solid steel bar welded to the other. It could be used to twist the bars on a cell window until they break in order to escape. Nash and I didn't want Kentucky to go with us because he was only eighteen and was serving a seven-year sentence called a "Youth Act." He only had to serve two years, do two years on parole, and then stay out of trouble for the remaining three and his conviction would disappear from his record. We had met with Kentucky a week earlier and convinced him his best interest would be served by not going. So we were set. At final count, Demerol, Nash, and I would rack in into Demerol's house, since he lived on the lower tier. We would stuff our beds to look like we were asleep.

Then, just as quickly as it all came together, the plan began to fall apart. Drug deal conflicts had erupted into a brutal fight the day before, ending with three in the infirmary. Nash had a friend who was the warden's clerk, and he sent word that a shakedown was coming to K-Unit to find drugs and weapons. We headed to the yard to tell Demerol so he could remove the bar breaker from his house. He said he had stashed it in Kentucky's cell. Nash and I were pissed. Demerol went and found Kentucky, and they came back to the yard.

Then, with hundreds of inmates cheering them on, they hit the fences right then, in broad daylight. Not smart.

As Demerol and Kentucky went down, everyone in the yard started screaming at the tower guard and throwing things. "The prison is in lockdown. Return to your cells," began blaring over and over on the PA system. Most headed in, but about fifty men remained behind until the guards came to escort them either to their cells or to the hole.

I went to my cell, locked in, sat down, and cried. Kentucky was a good kid. Demerol was an idiot. I could hear the guys walking into the unit laughing and talking about how awesome it was.

The lockdown was lifted around an hour and a half later. We quickly learned that Demerol was indeed dead, but Kentucky was in the prison hospital. I was still angry with Demerol even though he was dead. I kept thinking how selfish it was of him to put the kid in that position.

No one could remember the last time an escapee had been killed busting out of Lompoc Prison. Even the old timers who had been there for years said it wasn't typical. The guards would usually just pop off a couple of shots over the escapees' heads, then go out in the trucks and retrieve them as they emerged from the ring of eucalyptus trees that encircled the prison so thoroughly that after a few months prisoners tended to forget they were in the desert and felt like they were in a forest.

The next afternoon, Dr. Bliss, the prison psychiatrist, made arrangements for Nash and me to visit Kentucky at his hospital bed. Seeing his leg with rods and cables holding it together had a devastating effect on me. When I was still in county jail up in Seattle, Washington, three people—Max, Parker, and Music—had moved me toward a better direction without knowing it, but this incident woke me up to the realization of how fragile life can be.

Parker was a guard who had told me, "John, you are a good man. You're young and have your whole life ahead of you. It's not too late. Find something you are good at and apply yourself." Within twenty minutes of Parker's words, John Thomas Music, a death-row inmate, had said virtually the same thing to me. And then Max, an artist, gave me some markers and colored pencils and inspired me to start developing my gift of writing poems.

But it took Kentucky getting shot for me to begin to feel a true remorse for the people I had endangered throughout my escapades as a bank robber. I began to feel the weight of my actions.

Although I really didn't know who God was, I started thanking Him I hadn't shot anyone during any of the 157 robberies I had pulled. I also became afraid. Afraid that I wouldn't make it out of prison alive. It wasn't so much a fear of someone harming me but more a guilt of what I had done and the feeling that death was what I deserved.

Could I ever put it right?

Would I get out of this place alive?

And if I did, would I ever really be "free"?

CHAPTER ONE

SEARCHING

It was mid-1973, the beginning of my third year of incarceration. I decided to stop doing drugs and begin the process of working on presenting a better face to the parole board, which I would be seeing in a little over 18 months.

I needed to clean up my act a bit, which meant no more drugs. I wasn't into smoking dope; it made me paranoid. Seriously, one toke and everyone around me instantly became a nark. My drug of choice was LSD, or acid, as it was called. I was pretty regular with it and I spent most weekends traveling to wherever my microdot took me.

So I told my best friend Paul Stavenjord, "I'm not going to do anymore LSD. I need to concentrate on getting out of here."

Yet Paul insisted, "When we get out, you at least need to smoke a joint with me to celebrate." I promised.

During my first two years in prison I had witnessed rapes, murder, escapes, riots, and suicides. I hadn't found God behind the prison walls, but I was certainly searching. For what, I didn't know.

I was reading nearly everything I could get my hands on, especially if it had to do with Eastern religion. Paul Stavenjord and I had shaved our heads and were spending time on the prison yard meditating and chanting by a small altar where we placed oranges and apples as offerings to the combination Hindu, Buddhist, and Taoist god we had concocted. Paul was into it much more than I was. I was just glad to have a true friend, someone I could trust. (And I found LSD combined with Kundalini yoga was beyond amazing.)

Other than studying religions and working out on the weights in the yard, I mostly practiced guitar. My grandmother, Nanny, had bought me a guitar the first year I was here. When it arrived, however, I opened the package to find a small, almost toy-sized, baby-blue guitar with cactuses painted on it. Nanny didn't know any better so I couldn't hold it against her. I did, however, have to scramble in order to get it into the trash before anyone saw me with it. Merely owning something looking like that could mean danger or even death in here.

A few weeks later, Nick Nash loaned me a guitar he'd had for a few months but never played. I was blessed to be able to keep it as long as I wanted. Nash was a great guy.

I had grown up listening to Led Zeppelin and The Beatles but there was something about Linda Ronstadt's voice that swayed me over to country music. Then Credence Clearwater Revival and the Eagles sealed the deal. I had become a country music fan. Then along came Merle Haggard. His songs about prison spoke to my condition, as they say.

I was also working for Barbara Bliss, the staff psychiatrist who pulled me out of the flames of destruction. We went over my childhood and my life of crime, turning over every detail, no matter how small, hoping to discover and correct everything that might have led to the choices I had made.

I had become increasingly disenchanted with the concept of rehabilitation. I trusted nothing within the system except Dr. Bliss. My caseworker, R. R. Kelly, taught me how to beat the system, but I wanted to become a better person. What good does it do you to get out if you just end up back in because you are stuck in the same old routine? I seriously wanted to be able to get out and stay out. I concluded that rehabilitation was something you did in spite of the system, not because of it.

I enjoyed working for Dr. Bliss. She gave me a key to her office and I could go in there right after breakfast and make coffee before she came in. I read several of her books about psychiatry and counseling. I started teaching counseling classes, such as Re-evaluation Therapy, Transactional Analysis, and Carkhuff, Gestalt, and Behavioral Counseling. Then I was promoted to the board of directors of the Peer Counseling Program.

Barb determined that my desire for a mother's love and the lack of a father figure had resulted in my perceived need to win love from my mother by showering gifts upon her. Barb said, "Your mother doesn't love you and as long as you fight that, you will be in bondage and you will be unable to move on in life. You need to accept the fact that you are not, and perhaps will never be, loved by her." I struggled with her conclusions but took it as a necessary pill to bring about my healing.

Through recommendations from Dr. Bliss and my caseworker, my custody level was reduced from maximum to medium, and I was accepted into B-Unit, the prison honor unit. The cool thing about B-Unit was that you actually had a key to your cell and you could be in or out of your house during count times, as long as you were within the unit. You could stay up—and even out—as late as you wanted, as long as you made it to work on time.

Within a few months I began working with a program called Two-Way Street. On my twenty-first birthday, my custody status was once again reduced—this time to minimum. After training, we were taken out of the facility four days a week to a center in Santa Barbara that worked with people who were mentally disabled. We did Behavioral Modification and Behavioral Counseling. By today's standards, these techniques are considered cruel and dehumanizing but at the time they were groundbreaking.

November 23, 1973

I sat alone in my cell listening to
Merle Haggard sing, *"Mama tried . . . I turned 21 in prison . . ."*

CHAPTER TWO

FEDERAL PRISON CAMP

"Hope and your future are the fences that keep you from running."

In my fourth year I was transferred to the prison camp. The camp was a federal facility on twenty acres just outside of the prison. No fences and no gun towers.

Shortly after my transfer, some of the Watergate conspirators began arriving. Daniel Segretti was the first. They called him the trickster. He worked for Nixon pulling pranks on the democrats. Not the cute type of pranks. More like things that made them look stupid and gullible.

Next, Nixon's events coordinator, Mr. Berg, showed up. Finally G. Gordon Liddy arrived. He was Nixon's personal lawyer. Berg's bunk was next to mine, and late each evening, Segretti and Liddy would meet up with him and talk late into the night. Within a few weeks, Liddy was transferred to some other facility back East.

By the end of 1974, I had finished two years of college math courses at UCSB. I had also aced the final exam in an extended HVAC vocational training course and had a central file stuffed with various certificates from the counseling classes I had both taken and taught. I managed to stay out of the hole and, in fact, it had been more than a year since I had been written up for anything.

It was time for my parole hearing. Dr. Bliss told me that the parole board rules had been modified to allow inmates to bring a representative to their parole hearing. You could bring another inmate, an attorney, a family member, or a staff member. I asked if she would represent me, and she said yes.

I had a long conversation with her about a parole plan. In the early '70s, the federal system allowed parole plans to include either your hometown of record or your place of conviction. For me, that would have been either Dallas, Texas or Seattle, Washington. Dallas was flooded with family members and I knew no one in Seattle. I picked the great Northwest, partially because I wasn't looking forward to rehashing my life in front of my family.

My stepfather Walt had given me some terrible advice when I was arrested, saying, "John, you need to count your whole family as dead. You have become the black sheep of the family, and no one will be here for you. They will either be making excuses for you or they will flat out forget that you exist. And when you do get out, if you expect support from them and don't find it, you will fail. That's why so many end up going back to prison."

As appalling as his advice was, I took it. For the most part, my family became more like acquaintances, people I knew but wasn't close to. My grandmother, Nanny, would write me, as did my Aunt Toni. But most didn't. My older brother, Donnie, visited me twice. However, I learned that Mom and Walt were traveling through Lompoc twice when I was serving my time there yet didn't stop by to see me.

So I mostly picked Seattle because I felt like I didn't have a family but also because I needed to prove something to myself. I needed to know I could make it, that I could survive without leaning on anyone. I needed to see if I was a man.

Both Barb and my caseworker, Kelly, said I shouldn't get my hopes up about parole because the odds were against me getting out on the first hearing. They both expected me to get set off at least a year, perhaps even two.

Barb said, "Hope for the best, expect the worse, and accept anything in between." That seemed to be the most common sentiment for facing the parole board.

While Kelly's words were a bit more pragmatic, they were clouded with cynicism. He said, "John, if you get your hopes up and are let down, I'm afraid you'll end up blowing all your progress. I don't want you to wind up in the hole. Or, worse yet, on suicide watch. There's also the strong probability that if you are denied, you'll be transferred back inside the walls."

It was three weeks until my scheduled appearance. So there was still plenty of time to worry.

Letters from Nanny had tapered off. It was more my fault than hers. I both enjoyed and hated hearing from Nanny. She would tell me all the cool things that were going on in the real world, and I would write back, "Everything here is the same. I get up. I go to sleep. I get bored." I had nothing to give her. Nothing changed from day to day. Nothing happened of interest to people on the outside. I had no news to report. So I had found myself answering every other letter.

With one week until my parole hearing, I woke up at 2:00 A.M. to the sound of voices in the other end of the dorm. Someone had smuggled a prostitute into the facility, and for $10 green each, she was taking on the whole dorm. I was invited to join in but declined. I think everyone except me and the Watergate boys had a go at her.

Because of the Watergate boys, our prison was getting a bad rap in the newspapers. They were reporting that Lompoc was a country club for the rich and influential. Soon the world viewed all of Lompoc prison through the lens of the prison camp. And even worse, they exaggerated the conditions. "There are golf courses and tennis courts. No one is locked in. They have free rein throughout the facility." There was no golf course, just a small putting green for practice. The tennis court had potholes and cracks in the cement, and the netting was worn and full of holes. People within the prison became highly offended when their treatment was painted as pampered.

December 25, 1974

"It was Christmas in prison and the food was real good.
We had turkey and pistols carved out of wood."
"Christmas in Prison," John Prine, © 1973

CHAPTER THREE

THE PAROLE BOARD

January 20, 1975

Barb summoned me to her office the morning of my parole board hearing. We were scheduled for shortly after 12:00 P.M. Even though living in the camp meant fewer restrictions, going back into the prison meant handcuffs and a guard. I entered through the sally port to the yard, and the sound of its clanging giant doors had a heart-stopping tone. I wasn't surprised about the cuffs, but I was curious about why they kept them on until I was in front of Barb's office.

"Are you ready for this?" she questioned.

"As ready as I can be," came my answer.

"Remember, don't get your hopes up."

"Too late for that." I was almost bubbly.

We spent the morning going over details of my parole plan and tweaking each line to make sure it was precise and not too wordy.

At noon we walked down the corridor to the administrative wing and took a seat in the hall. Just one more inmate, then we would be called.

There was a clandestine approach to the parole board's findings. You meet with two parole judges, and then a third judge who is back in Washington D.C. reviews the file and tape from the hearing. He casts his (sometimes deciding) vote. You need two out of three votes to receive parole.

If both judges you meet with vote no, they tell you no and give you a date when you can reapply. This is called a set off. If one votes yes and the other votes no, they give you a provisional parole date. If both vote yes, they still give you a provisional date, because they don't want you to know where they stand. Doesn't make much sense to me.

Barb stood up and looked through the small window in the door to the office where they were holding the parole hearings. As she turned around, I saw she was smiling.

"Someone other than me is smiling on you, John. Looks like good news."

Puzzled, I asked, "What do you mean?"

"See the judge on the right? I worked for him in the private sector when he was an attorney, and I was in forensic psychiatry."

"Well, that's one," I assumed.

"It gets better," she added.

"How?"

"See the other judge? I dated him years ago."

"I hope you left on good terms?" I questioned.

"Indeed we did. He moved to D.C. as an aide to a senator."

But still. Who knows? I didn't find much hope. I guess I'd taken Barb and Kelly's advice more to heart than I realized.

"Look, John. I'm not saying you should get your hopes up. I'm simply saying we have a better shot than we did an hour ago."

When we were finally called in, it was like old home week. Both judges jumped to their feet and greeted Barb.

Then they each said to the other, "*You* know Barbara?"

It was as if I didn't even exist. They noticed me after a couple of minutes of hugs and handshakes.

One of them said, "Have a seat, Mr. Swanger."

"Thank you," I said and sat down. Barb also took a seat.

Then one of them asked her, "Is Mr. Swanger ready to reenter society?"

She responded, "John has worked hard to find out the root of his errant ways, and I believe he will make a positive impact on humanity. His chances of re-offending are minimal. In fact, I'd stake my reputation on it."

At that point, I was asked to wait outside. As I left the room, all the hugs and handshakes re-commenced. I peeked through the window and watched as they handed Barb a piece of paper.

I heard her thank them, and they all said their goodbyes. As Barb exited, she handed me the paper. It was marked with a provisional parole date a few months away.

Barb said, "Don't worry about the provisional. You are going home, John. They both said yes." Then she added, "Try to contain yourself. It's best that no one knows that we know for sure. Just wait until you receive the final word from the panel."

I thought keeping quiet would be easy, because I was having a hard time believing it myself. Even if it were true, I was certain something, somehow, would go wrong, and I would be waiting forever.

I headed back to my bunk and turned the radio on. For the next two hours, I sat dreaming about the outs and hoping I was actually getting nearer to my dream. I also wondered, *With so many great songs, why are the two Credence Clearwater Revival songs about rain my favorites?* I thought of "Who'll Stop the Rain," and "Have You Ever Seen the Rain?" Perhaps I was destined for Seattle.

CHAPTER FOUR

THE ANSWER

Mail call—and the only letter I had wasn't even a letter, just a memo. But oh, what a memo it was.

The very first line boldly said, "You have been issued a seven-month parole date. You will be transferred to serve the final 90 days of your incarceration at a federal halfway house."

"The Bishop Lewis House is located at 703 8th Ave. in Seattle, Washington. You will be placed on a bus in Lompoc and delivered to the Seattle bus terminal. It is your responsibility to make your way to the halfway house. Failure to do so in a timely manner will result in immediate and complete revocation of your parole, with the issuance of an arrest warrant for your capture and return to custody, along with an additional charge of 18 U.S.C. §751 and 752, Escape from Federal Custody."

I was ecstatic, overwhelmed, and, to be honest, I was an emotional wreck. I headed back to my bunk and just cried.

Barbara summoned me, and once again I was taken inside the prison and cuffed at the gate.

The guard said, "Don't worry, you are not in trouble. It's just policy."

I told him, "I know." I couldn't stop grinning for the entire walk through the sally port, the yard, and down the corridor to Barb's office.

Barb was standing at the door and hugged me as the guard removed the cuffs. Once again I began to cry. I couldn't help it. I was so grateful for all she had done for me from our first meeting, when she told me she wasn't used to inmates asking to see her, through all the sessions where we hashed through my life looking for answers. Not to mention representing me at the parole board.

I said, "Dr. Bliss, there is no way I could ever thank you enough. You have saved my life. I have no way to repay you for what you have done."

She replied, "Yes, you can, John. Stay out. If you come back, it's the same as telling me I wasted my time with you. I don't think that's the case, though."

With that, she pulled out my file and said, "I want to read something to you."

She dug through and finally pulled out a single paper. "John, let me quote a couple of friends you have met along your way."

With that, she read to me what Parker and Music told me while I was in King County Jail, about having my whole life ahead of me. She said, "It's true, John. It's not too late. You have also found something you are good at. Now go and apply yourself."

Then she added, "You, John Swanger, are a writer. You have a way with words that is captivating and illuminating. You are in a rare breed of people who have the ability to paint pictures with your words. People don't just read what you write, they find themselves living within your stories."

I told her, "I don't know if I can write beyond myself."

Barb replied, "The gift is within you. It might be for writing books or songs, but you defiantly have the gift."

"Thank you," I said.

As I was leaving to head back to the camp, she said, "When you come by on your merry-go-round I have a present for you."

"If you have faith as a grain of mustard seed, you shall say to this mountain, Remove hence to yonder place; and it shall remove; and nothing shall be impossible to you."
Matthew 17:20

My friend John Miranda had written a play called *Mustard Seeds* about a guy in prison struggling with life and dealing with the everyday problems that prison life throws at you. I auditioned and got the part of Mr. Bertacelli, a cynical parole judge. We performed the play for the entire prison population and then performed a special viewing for the staff. After a standing ovation, we were treated to a catered dinner served by the upper staff of the prison. Some of them were quite moved by the play's emotional honesty.

There were a few people in attendance from outside of the facility. We learned that one of them was a producer for a talent agency in Hollywood and another was a writer for a newspaper. Within a few days, we received copies of a newspaper article. Beyond the great reviews of the talent and production, it raved about the message that *Mustard Seeds* carried: prisoners are real people with shady pasts but with hopes for the future. It shed light on the disregard some staff and authorities have for the convicts.

Afterward, Miranda told me that writing and sharing his play was the greatest feeling he had ever had. "Just getting the message out that we are humans. Lost, misguided, broken, and often self-destructive—but humans still."

I told him, "You know, some day you'll be released, and you will feel a much stronger joy than even this."

His reply was instant. "John, not even a full pardon would feel as good, knowing that finally, for the first time in my life, someone heard me. Someone listened."

Miranda had, in just a few words, conveyed to me what it was I had always longed for. What I had spent my childhood searching for. "Thank you," I said without realizing what I was saying.

"For what?"

"For being real, and for being my friend."

I was the only cast member in the camp. The rest were behind the walls. But two weeks later, without explanation, the entire cast and crew of *Mustard Seeds* was transferred to the camp except for Diego, who was in the hole for attempting to escape. Miranda was summoned to Warden Kenton's office. When he returned he called us all together.

"We have been invited to do *Mustard Seeds* for the California Parole Commission next month, on the Queen Mary in Long Beach."

Everyone was excited. Someone asked, "What about Diego?"

Miranda said, "We have to find a replacement. Kenton gave me a list of guys with minimum custody that could be transferred to the camp as soon as we find one suitable for Diego's role as John Paul."

"Anyone on the list that we know?" I asked.

"I know a couple of them, but trust me, we don't want either of them trying to act."

The next two weeks, Miranda spent most of each day inside running auditions. Finally he said he had found someone. Andy Coakley was in for wire fraud and was due to flat time his ticket in three months.

Andy came to the camp just two days later. Rehearsals began as soon as he unpacked. But things weren't going so well until Miranda decided to switch roles and plug Andy into a different one. This was the fix we all needed. Rehearsals smoothed out and before long we were ready to roll.

We headed out early the morning of the production. Cast and crew, 15, along with six prison-staff members including both the warden, Frank Kenton, and the assistant warden, Thomas Koehane. We headed in two large vans down Highway 1 to Gaviota, where we picked up the Coastal Highway 101 and continued south to Long Beach.

Spontaneously, we all started singing "Lodi" along with Credence Clearwater Revival on the radio. We were a bit surprised that Kenton was singing also. I guess we were a bit shocked to see him as a normal person. Strange.

As we were pulling into Long Beach, I could see the Queen Mary in the distance. It was, without a doubt, the largest ship I have ever seen— well over three football fields long and very imposing. They gave us brochures as we boarded telling us it was built in 1933 and had crossed the Atlantic a thousand times. It was bigger than the Titanic. I was impressed as well by its elegance and beauty, and was humbled to be acting in such an awesome venue.

We were escorted to our berths and given keys and dining passes. On the bunks in the berths were baskets with snacks and fruit. Hanging next to the bunks were white bathrobes with "RMS Queen Mary" embroidered on the pocket. I felt like I had died and gone to heaven. Even though the prison staff escorts entered before us and removed the two complimentary bottles of wine and the long-stemmed wine glasses.

We were told to leave our bags and report to the conference room two decks above for a meeting. At the meeting we were introduced to Thordis Brandt, a Hollywood actress and makeup artist. I found out Thordis was the ex-wife of James Arness, who played Marshall Matt Dillon on the TV show *Gunsmoke*. She was also John Miranda's girlfriend. We also met two very attractive female reporters from Los Angeles.

The crew was sent to the dining hall for dinner while Thordis did make up for the other actors. Mine took longer because she had to make me look much older. As soon as our makeup and hair were done, we headed down to the dining room for dinner. Although our cards allowed for anything on the menu, the warden told us not to order the lobster. He said he would never hear the end of it once the other inmates found out.

The steaks were great and as well the burgundy sauce that went with them.

Miranda said, "Let's hurry. We need to get to the stage and get a close up feel for what we are up against."

Ted asked for a to-go box, and I thought the waiters were going to come unglued. "Sir," they said, "your meal card isn't for dinner only; it's for anything during your entire stay. If you need anything else, just ring the kitchen."

Ted said "Okay," then wrapped the leftover steak in his napkin and shoved it in his pocket. I guess prison habits are hard to break.

We all met on the stage and Miranda ran through some of his scenes and made adjustments. Then we all went backstage to wardrobe where, for the first time in a few years, I was dressed in civilian clothes. I had a dark grey suit and a tie. New black loafers and black socks. I looked sharp. Most of the guys were dressed in regular prison attire—khakis and cheap brown leather shoes. Miranda made sure his were a wrinkled and slightly worn set.

He said, "I want to make them feel the full impact."

CHAPTER FIVE

THE SHOW MUST GO ON

The play started. From backstage I could see that even before things barely got rolling, the audience was really getting into it. At times, the applause was almost disruptive as an actor's lines were inaudible or delayed.

While none of us were veterans at acting, it was obvious that large portions of the crowd weren't at all experienced with attending an on-stage production.

At one point I wondered if the applause was genuine or perhaps a sort of twisted, sarcastic sense of humor. Maybe these were people who didn't want to attend but were compelled by their supervisors. Either way, I began to feel uneasy with my scene. I wasn't comfortable at all. It wasn't so much stage fright as a desire not to be made fun of.

Miranda, between his scenes, came by where I was sitting and tried to encourage me. "I don't know if they are genuinely applauding or not, but I know this: our job is to put the best product we can on the table. If they take it, fine. If not, at least we are going home with our dignity intact."

To me, the call to the stage was similar to my experience grabbing the front door of a bank for a robbery. It was a place of decision. A crossing over the point of no return. All the butterflies went away. The fear was in the anticipation and the anguish of knowing I could back out; the relief was in the deciding that I was in, there would be no turning back now.

Between acts, I took my place onstage and waited for the curtain to re-open. Miranda was just off stage and he was giving me the thumbs up. As the curtains drew apart, he walked on and took his seat. We each went through our dialogs without a hitch. It was scripted for me, "Mr. Bertacelli," to dismiss him without any indication of a favorable outcome.

Mr. Bertacelli: "Thank you, Jason. Please send the next inmate in."

Jason turns and walks to the door, but before exiting, he turns back and says, "Mr. Bertacelli?"

"Yes, Jason?"

"We are real people. With real lives."

"I know that, Jason. Now please send the next inmate in."

The only time I went off script was when Jason turned back to look at me again; I reached back to the stack of files and grabbed his from the top, as if I had already forgotten him and had to remind myself of his name. "Yes . . . Jason?" Again there was applause.

Once off stage, Miranda said to me, "John, today you graduated from being an actor who simply takes direction to one who knows how to own the part."

"I don't think acting is what I am supposed to do with my life," I replied

"Yes, but it's cool to know you can," he replied.

All our fears of the audience being sarcastic began to fade as the ovation continued. Miranda added, "Cynicism is a strange thing. It comes at you from all directions. However, tonight I think the cynicism we witnessed was our own."

Once the play was over, Miranda went out for a curtain call. He took a bow, then motioned for us all to come out. It was exciting.

Miranda stayed back to talk to the reporters while the rest of us headed to the dining room to have the hors d'oeuvres the kitchen had prepared for us. Warden Kenton and A.W. Koehane met us there to debrief. They congratulated us and applauded our performance. Then, once again, they went over their expectations for the evening. Kenton said, "You can hang out in the fourth deck social room until 11:30 P.M., but then it's back to your berths for the remainder of the night."

Koehane added, "No visiting other berths and no one allowed into your berths."

We waited for Miranda, then hung out for another hour eating little slices of bread with tiny black fish eggs on them, topped with green onions and little sprigs of rosemary. They also served slices of cucumber with smoked salmon on top. I loved the salmon but the fish eggs were way too salty for me.

"It's an acquired taste," Miranda said.

I came back, "Why bother?"

The knock at my door startled me. I jumped to my feet to see one of the guards peering into and around my berth as well my bunk.

He said, "Grab your things and come into the hall."

"What's going on?" I asked.

He didn't respond, just backed out of the door. Once outside I could see they had Ted in handcuffs. We were all escorted to the vans and packed mostly into one of them, while Ted and three guards were in the other.

"What's up, Miranda?" I asked.

"They caught Ted in bed with one of the reporters this morning," he replied.

The journey back to Lompoc was not as joyful as the trip out. We arrived and Ted was immediately taken to the hole.

Koehane called us all to his office and said, "There will be a full investigation."

He then asked if any of us had anything to contribute to the report.

Almost in unison we responded, "No, sir."

With that he quipped, "I didn't think so."

We left his office and were escorted back to the camp.

Miranda called us all to his bunk and told us, "I am really pissed. Even though Ted is my best friend, he jeopardized the entire program."

Andy said, "Not really. He was busted after the show. So, no harm, no foul."

Miranda, even more angry, snapped, "You think it was over? This, Coakley, is just the beginning. I didn't set my sights on the California Parole Commission. I'm looking much higher and further down the road."

I laid down on my bunk and turned my radio on. Linda Ronstadt began to capture my heart with her "Silver Threads and Golden Needles."

Within few days we learned that one of the other guys had snuck into one of the reporter's berths. But unlike Ted, he was smart enough to turn in alone before morning.

CHAPTER SIX

....

THE MERRY-GO-ROUND

My last three months in the camp seemed to drag on forever. But finally the day came for me to do the merry-go-round. That's the day before your "walk out," when you show up at administration and pick up a form with a list of a dozen or so check boxes on each side. Up to twenty-four checkpoints throughout the prison need to sign off or you don't get released.

I started making the rounds. It is said to strictly be a check-off process but, in reality, it's almost like a going-away salute. You go to each department so they can indicate you are clear and not owing any property, but generally each department head signs his name and adds a "Good Luck" or "Congratulations" within the department's assigned box.

Administration was the first to sign off. From there I left and headed to the captain's office, then the Meritorious Service Award office where they told me I had a $25 meritorious service award from the mental health department. They told me it would be sent to Receiving & Discharge and I would get it when I was released. On to the commissary where I had $38 on the books, which they also said I would receive upon release. Then to the hole. Then to the library and the school. I had to stop by B-Unit to show I had actually turned in the key from when I was assigned there. Same with K-Unit to show there wasn't any missing property from my time there.

I returned to camp, gathered my uniforms and bedding, and hurried down the corridor to the laundry to turn in all my clothing and receive a set just for the night, then on to central supply where I turned in my pillow and blankets. They, too, gave me a set for the night.

I headed to the chow hall for lunch and hung out with the kitchen staff in the back. Mr. Connolly signed off on my record. I had worked for him in the kitchen when I first arrived at Lompoc. He said, "You know, the more you push yourself, the further you will go. There is nothing you can't achieve if you apply yourself."

Next was what I had been looking forward to. Dr. Bliss was smiling as I walked through the door. She stood and hugged me. "It's been a long time coming, John, but it certainly has been worth the wait. Right?"

I just nodded and tried to smile, but it turned into a grin.

Barb said, "Before I forget, I have a gift for you. But you have to promise you won't show it to anyone. And if you are found with it, promise me you'll not let on you got it from me. "

With that she opened a manila file folder and handed me two 8 x 10 color, glossy, aerial photos of the prison. I turned them over and on the back they were stamped *Classified*.

She said, "I'm not real sure who God is, and I'm not certain I would submit my life to Him if I did. But I believe in the power of having faith in yourself." She added, "You know the concept of Alcoholics Anonymous, right?"

I replied, "Yes."

She pointed at the photo and said, "Use this. Let this be your higher power. Keep this handy and rely on it to help you refrain from anything that might lure you into a life that will end up back in here."

We spent the next hour remembering our journey together, and when it was time to go, I began to cry. No one had helped me adjust my path more than Barb.

As I walked out I said, "I love you, Dr. Bliss."

She said, "I love you, too, John."

I walked out trying to compose myself. I didn't want anyone to see I had been crying.

From there, I went outside to the industries buildings. I had actually worked at several of them earlier in my stay. I stopped into the sign factory. There I had worked in silk screening and as well the tool room. We made street signs and license plates. Mr. Canterra signed off on me.

Next I went to the electronic cable factory, where many of the wiring harnesses for the space program were made. The supervisor there was new so I didn't know him from when I had worked there three years earlier. However, he offered me his congratulations and more. "Are you a believer?" he asked.

I replied, "I suppose I am. I believe in a lot of things."

"But are you a believer in Jesus?"

"I can say I don't disbelieve in Him."

As he was scribbling his name on my sheet, he said, "Every person that gets out of here has the same chance of making it on the outside. But if you allow Him, Jesus will walk with you and guide you along your path."

I said, "I suppose He might. But I'm not sure I believe He would want to help me. I haven't been the best example of someone who deserves His help."

He handed the form back to me and said, "Psalm 91. Do you have a Bible?"

I replied, "No."

"Proverbs 3:5-6," he added. "Find a Bible and look them up."

I thanked him and left. Next I went into the print shop where I saw John Battistella, the head printer. I'd gotten to know him when I worked there for quite a bit of my time, and also through the school where he taught music. He was an accomplished musician. More precisely, a saxophonist. He had told me earlier on that he couldn't teach me much on the guitar but he could help me learn to read music. The first time I walked into his office, I brought my harmonica with me. He called it a "dime store saxophone."

I handed him my paper and asked him to sign off on it.

He said, "Will you let me tell you a story first?"

I had always liked hanging out with him and listening as he shared memories from his eighty-plus years.

So I replied, "You bet!"

"Of course you know I play the sax. What you may not know is that I was once part of a forty-piece swing band. We traveled all over America doing live shows. One day, one of the band members called a meeting while our band leader was out. We discussed how we were all frustrated with the roads and concluded that the reason we weren't gaining success was because of our leader. We were convinced we needed to fire him and find someone more talented. We voted, and that day we fired our director, Lawrence Welk."

"Wow," I mumbled.

Mr. Battistella said, "Obviously, Mr. Welk went on to become one of the most famous band leaders of all time, and here I am working in a prison." He continued, "The point is, a man's heart can deceive him all his days. Proverbs 16:25 says, 'There's a way that seems right unto a man, but the end thereof are the ways of death.'"

I asked him what Proverbs 3:5-6 was.

"It's the same thing I am trying to tell you. John, the main thing you need to get is: you can't always trust John. 'Trust in the LORD with all of your heart. Lean not on your own understanding. Acknowledge Him [Jesus] in all your ways, and He will direct your steps.'"

As I was walking out the door, Mr. Battistella said, "Good luck, John. I'll pray for you."

From there I walked to the sally port and showed them the merry-go-round form. They raised the massive gate and let me out. I walked the quarter mile back to the prison camp and lay down on my bunk. Somewhere between Golden Earring singing "Radar Love" and Deep Purple's "Smoke on the Water," I fell asleep.

CHAPTER SEVEN

FREEDOM

My eyes opened exactly two minutes before the morning bell. It was 5:58 A.M., and I was up and grabbing for my trousers. As I pulled them on, I watched the other prisoners tossing and turning in their bunks and cussing the day. I supposed no one would listen if I told them it was a great day. So I didn't.

I unplugged my radio and handed it to Gomez, a drug smuggler from Mazatlán. I shoved my harmonicas into my bag along with my journals and my poems. Then I emptied my locker of all the commissary and just sat it on top for whoever wanted it. I wrote my padlock combination on a piece of masking tape, stuck it to the back, and handed the lock to Wilson, who still had a few months to serve on his drug charges. I grabbed my cassette player and laid it on the foot of Douglass's bunk, as he was still asleep. Finally, I grabbed the guitar my friend Nick Nash had loaned me two years earlier. He said I could use it as long as I wanted because he wasn't getting anywhere with learning to play it.

I shared several pats on the back and hugs with several other inmates as well as the staff. Lots of "Good lucks" and "Congrats" came my way. Then I headed to the prison's sally port so I could turn in my merry-go-round and make my exit.

Finally it was here, the time for my "walk out."

I entered the main building and turned left to stop by K-Unit to drop off Nash's guitar.

"You keep it," Nash said. "You'll get a lot more use out of it than I ever will."

"Are you sure?" I queried. "It's such a nice guitar."

"I want you to have it, John. Just promise me you'll wear it out."

"Thanks a bunch. Will do," I said as I was leaving.

I stopped by Mr. Kelly's office for my final signature and to turn in the form. He started shaking my hand, and he couldn't stop talking about our time over the past four years.

"John," he said, "it has truly been an honor to know you and work with you. Please do me a favor and make something of yourself."

I thanked him.

Then he added, "In my line of work, it's rare to actually see someone you truly believe can make it. You, John, are that one for me."

We walked to the Receiving and Discharge wing and I was given the box of my things they'd put on the shelf nearly four years earlier. I opened it and saw my wallet, along with my expired Texas driver's license, my draft card, and my Social Security card. There were a couple of photos, including the one of my Aunt Toni. They'd long ago thrown away the clothing I was arrested in, but they gave me a T-shirt and a white dress shirt that didn't fit, and a pair of dress slacks. Black loafers and black socks. They asked me if I wanted a tie. I declined. Finally, they handed me a cheap grey windbreaker.

I had to sign a stack of papers, including my directions once I arrived in Seattle, and a form that said I agreed never to possess a gun or any other dangerous weapon. There was also a form that said I agreed never to enter into an agreement with any law enforcement agency to be an informant or undercover operative. Then they handed me a bus ticket to Seattle, a sack lunch, a bottle of orange juice, and some cash. Between the 25-dollar Meritorious Service Award, my 38-dollar commissary, and the standard 125 dollars walkout money, I was leaving with nearly 200 dollars. The Pink Floyd song "Money" started going through my mind.

I was actually getting a bit nervous. My guilty conscious had always haunted me. *Do I deserve to be getting out? If something could go wrong, it probably will.*

Mr. Kelly said a final goodbye and the Receiving and Discharge guard walked me to the gate. I was disappointed that, instead of getting to walk out like in the movies and the fact that they call it a *Walk Out*, I was loaded into a van and driven out.

They took me to the Greyhound station in town and dropped me off. I waited twenty minutes until my bus was called, and I boarded. The bus was mostly empty except for a few people sitting near the front, a young Mexican couple, and a couple of drunk old men.

The driver said, "We will be pulling out in just a few minutes. Just waiting for one more passenger."

CHAPTER EIGHT

WHAT ARE THE ODDS?

Once again my paranoia and my guilty conscience were thinking, *Perhaps they aren't waiting for another passenger at all. Perhaps there's been a mistake and they are really coming to get me and take me back.*

I was shocked to see the passenger who boarded next. Of all the people in the area, and of the more than fifteen hundred inmates in Lompoc, the one person who walked through the door and headed to the back was my best friend from prison, Paul Stavenjord.

"What the heck, Paul?!" I shouted. "Didn't expect to see you here!"

"I was actually supposed to get out yesterday, but there was a problem with my merry-go-round, and my clearance from Alaska didn't come through until this morning."

"Not only the same release date and time, but riding the same bus to Seattle? Amazing," I said.

"Not really so shocking. I am going to Alaska and my ride has to go through Seattle." Paul took a seat across the aisle from me and threw his bag under the seat in front of him.

The door closed and we finally began to pull out of the station. I started to think back on the latter stages of my time as a robber. The more I robbed, the more I began to fear getting caught or, worse yet, getting shot or shooting someone else. It became harder and harder to get out of the car and walk up to the bank. My nerves were frayed. My stomach would tighten up and I often felt like I was going to puke.

Somehow the door handle of the bank door became a switch that turned off the fear. I discerned it was a point of commitment, a point of no turning back. It was as if, up to the time I grabbed the door handle, I could always change my mind and back out. But once I touched the door, I was in.

It was the turmoil of having to decide that tortured me. I learned that and began approaching the bank or store more quickly so I wouldn't put my body through the stress. My hand on the door handle triggered a release of my inner tension. Oddly, through all the stress, I never backed out of a robbery.

The last time I felt that kind of relief was when I finally left Bill and Linda and headed back home. Somehow, crossing the Truckee River Bridge in Reno, Nevada, brought the same release. The roar of the bus engine brought with it a similar calming comfort, which I desperately needed.

I looked over at Paul and saw him rolling a joint. I thought, *He could very well be the first person ever to actually smuggle drugs* out *of a prison.* He asked if I had a light, and I handed him my matches. He lit up and offered the joint to me. I declined.

"You promised you would get high with me the day we get out," he proclaimed.

"Well, first off, in my defense, I had no idea at the time that we would both get out on the same day," I replied. "And, as well, I really don't want to jeopardize my freedom again."

"I understand."

"Perhaps the day I get off parole we might light one up together."

The whole joint thing led us into a lengthy conversation about everything we had witnessed during our years together in Lompoc. We spent the next few hours reliving the riots and lockdowns. The rapes and murders we had seen. The escapes. The friends we had watched come and go. We finally began to discuss the studies we'd shared. All the Eastern philosophies and faith we had embraced. Paul reached into his bag and offered some of his books on Buddhism to me.

"You know you'll need these if you plan to find a better path. One that leads you into a more peaceful and tranquil place," he said.

"You keep them, brother. I'll be okay. Plus, I am not allowed much space in the halfway house I'm heading to. I want to make sure I have room for my guitar."

I took my guitar from the overhead rack and showed it to Paul. "Nick gave me this," I said. He was blown away.

"It's a nice guitar, but an even nicer gift," he said.

"Have you ever thought about learning to play guitar?" I asked.

"No. I learned to play the flute in high school, but I like the recorder much more," he replied.

We continued on north with a few stops along the way. Mostly just five minutes here and there, but nothing where we could get off and stretch our legs. Then we pulled into the terminal at San Francisco.

The driver announced, "We will be here for an hour and fifteen minutes. Remember all the B's. You'll have time to grab a bite. Burgers, bacon, or bologna. But be sure to be back on the bus by the time we re-board. We don't want to leave anyone behind."

CHAPTER NINE

DOES ANYBODY REALLY KNOW WHAT TIME IT IS?

As we were getting off the bus, Paul said, "I've been craving pizza for years."

"I just want a burger. A good burger," I replied. "And then I need to find a few things."

"Like what?"

"I want a pocket watch like my grandfather used to carry. And a lighter," I said.

Right across the street from the station I saw a jewelry store, so I headed over. I asked the clerk for a pocket watch and he showed me a beauty.

He asked, "How much do you have to spend?"

"Five bucks," I replied.

"Sir, there is no such thing as a five-dollar pocket watch," he snapped and placed the watch back in the case.

I left and headed into the greasy spoon next door to get a burger. "One cheeseburger with everything, and fries to go, and a bottle of Coke, please."

A few minutes later and I was out the door. Next to the bus station was a Walgreens, so I went in. I asked about a lighter, and the lady handed me one. As I was looking at it I spotted, on the shelf behind her, a pocket watch. A Westclox with a black face.

"How much is that pocket watch?" I asked

"I'll check," she replied. "Looks like $4.50, but it comes with a chain."

"I'll take it. And the Zippo* also."

She bagged them both up. I thanked her and left. The watch was plain, nothing like the expensive gold-etched diamond one the jeweler had shown me, but it worked and it was cheap. Just what I wanted.

I was about to go into the bus terminal but decided to venture back across the street. I walked back into the jewelry store.

I proclaimed to the man behind the counter, "Here, sir, is what a five-dollar pocket watch looks like. Not nearly as fancy as yours, but it tells time and it was only $4.50."

With that, I left and boarded the bus. This time I was surprised to see the bus was nearly full. A Mexican lady had removed the "Occupied" placard from my seat and sat there with her child. I almost said something, but decided just to move over and sit with Paul. I grabbed my bag from under the seat and shoved it in next to Paul's.

I was looking forward to my burger, then the little girl across from me caught my eye. I could see she was eyeing my burger. I thought she looked hungry.

"Are you hungry? *¿Tienes hambre?*" I asked.

"*Sí.*"

"*Esta bueno?*" I asked her mom

"*Sí, Como no,*" she said

I handed her the burger and fries and watched as she removed the onions and started to eat.

"*Muchas gracias,*" the mother said.

"*De nada,*" I answered.

"To everything—turn, turn, turn, There is a season—turn, turn, turn and a time to every purpose under heaven. A time to give, a time to take."
© 1965 The Byrds

Paul said, "I got you covered, John. This is more pizza than I could eat on my own. Here, grab some."

---

*lighter

I ended up eating five slices to Paul's three.

We started hashing over our crimes that had landed us in prison. I had robbed a lot of places. Paul was in for state crimes, including robberies, in Alaska. There aren't prisons in Alaska, so they contract with the feds to house all their prisoners elsewhere.

The next two days passed, and finally we arrived in Seattle, Washington. I woke Paul and let him know it was time to say goodbye. I had enjoyed the trip, but honestly, I was pleased to be off the bus.

CHAPTER TEN

....

THE GREAT NORTH-WET

It started raining as I walked out of the Greyhound station. But I really didn't mind. Back in Lompoc, rain meant an immediate return to the building. No one was allowed on the yard at all. I think it was for security reasons. I looked at the mimeographed directions to the halfway house they had given me along with my release papers. I could still smell the ammonia from the purple ink.

I thought for just a second about calling a cab, but opted to walk the mile and a half up the hill. It was further than I had been allowed to walk in years. Freedom.

I found the Bishop Lewis House was actually an old mansion from the early '30s converted by the feds in the late '60s. I walked up to the desk and told them my name.

The guy behind the counter was about 45 years old and obviously gay. Not sort of gay, he was flaming. He had a handlebar moustache and plucked eyebrows.

He said, "Fourth door on the right, up the stairs, sweetie. Throw your stuff in your locker, then come back to me . . . for a pass."

I hurried up and was back in less than a minute.

As I was returning to the desk, he was signing someone out for the weekend.

"What kind of a pass?" I asked.

He said, "You are allowed to go back to town for an hour and a half to buy toiletries and anything else you need, but be back before 6:30 or you will be violated."

"Can I get a weekend pass?" I asked.

"No. Not until you have been here a while and the family members you will be staying with have been approved, if you have any."

He then handed me a form listing the dos and don'ts of the house as well as the locations of stores where I could shop. The dos included meal times and phone rules. The don'ts mostly addressed drugs, theft from other inmates, and fighting. Drinking was also strictly prohibited.

As I was heading out the door, he repeated, "Be sure to be back before 6:30. You don't want to get violated on your first night out."

I found myself walking faster, going down the hill back to town. Not because it was downhill but because I didn't want to waste time. It had stopped raining and for that I was glad.

Boy, was I ever in for a surprise when I got downtown. Four years earlier when I was arrested, I lived in a world where the guys chased the girls and if you were lucky, one would let you catch her. But, somehow, something they called "the sexual revolution" had happened while I was away. Everything had turned upside down.

As I walked into a bar and grill to order a burger, a very attractive waitress started eyeing me up. "You let me know if there is anything I can do for you," she said. "Anything."

I said, "I'll take a cheeseburger, fries, and a Coke." A few minutes later she brought my burger.

Again she said, "Are you sure there isn't anything else I can do for you? I get off at 6:00."

"I just got out of prison. I haven't been with a woman in four years. But I am in a halfway house and I'm due back there by 6:30. I would love to spend some time with you, but I just can't tonight," I said.

"Wait here." she said. She returned with a to-go box and said, "I'll drive you back." Apparently, she had clocked out early.

As we pulled into the halfway house, I asked, "Can I see you again?"

"Sorry, John, but this is what we call a short time but a good time. I already have someone who belongs to me."

With that I walked back into the Bishop Lewis house about twenty minutes late.

The flirty guy behind the counter said, "You know, I could send you right back to prison."

I was busy apologizing when he interrupted me and said, "I'm signing you in at 6:30, but remember—you owe me one."

I wasn't sure what he meant by "you owe me one," and I didn't want to know. I went up to my room, stuck the aerial photo of the prison on the wall, and started playing my guitar. I rolled a cigarette, sat back, and tried to relax.

I could begin to like the whole idea of girls chasing guys, I thought.

CHAPTER ELEVEN

ON PAPER

The weekend was spent sitting through orientation classes. Expansion of the dos and don'ts paper, plus classes on how to find a job. They suggested we not tell prospective employers about our crimes unless they specifically asked. And then we should try to minimize as much as possible. That didn't sound too smart to me. I thought it would be a much smarter idea to get it out of the way right off the bat. I didn't want to find a job, then be called into the office later and told, "Guess what we found out? You're fired."

I was also told I needed to report to my parole officer's office first thing Monday morning, a Mr. Garry Smith at the downtown federal building. They also gave us bus schedules and a 30-day bus pass.

Sunday morning, the house manager asked if I wanted to come down for the church services. I declined.

Monday morning I was at Mr. Smith's office a half-hour early. I was somewhat nervous about meeting the guy who would have my future in his hands for the next six years. However, that all went away within seconds after meeting him. He set me at ease when he pulled out a report Dr. Bliss had sent him.

He said, "Seems you have made quite an impression on our mutual friend, Barbara."

"I had no idea you knew her too," I responded.

"She is actually from Bainbridge Island, which is near here. She has worked with us on several cases over the years." He told me I would be expected to file a monthly report and come see him every week until I was released from the halfway house, and then come once every three months.

He concluded, "Other than that, just don't break any laws. Try to find a job."

I told him, "I need to find some clothes. Everything I have is on my back right now." He gave me a printout with the address of the Goodwill and a few other clothing banks in the area. It was helpful, but I said, "I am due back at the halfway house in thirty minutes so I'll have to find a way to get them to let me go."

"Let me give them a call." I waited out in the lobby while he called them.

He emerged and said, "You're free until eight this evening. Remember, no drinking." I thanked him and left.

I spent the rest of the morning at Goodwill and at a food and clothing bank called The Good Samaritan. Then I headed to Pike Street to see if the waitress I had met Friday was working. She wasn't but another equally pretty one was. Same, same.

Through playing pool in the clubs downtown I met a Filipino guy named David Morta. He was, without a doubt, the coolest guy I knew. He was a mechanic by trade and had an amazingly hot car. He was stylish and always dressed to the nines. He was a great pool player, but mostly he was a great dancer. Through him I learned how to dance. While my pool game was improving, my ladies game was overshadowing it. The '70s and the sexual revolution brought with it disco. And disco meant more babes. I was in.

We would go to dance clubs and ask girls to dance. Usually when we returned to our table we would find someone had bought us a drink, kind of a salute for controlling the dance floor. This was awesome because I was always pretty much broke. I only drank Coke but still, it was free. Great.

One evening I was at a club dancing and listening to the live band Soldier. I had just sat down when a young lady stopped at my table and asked me to dance. I did and she asked me to join her at her table. I told her I didn't have any money to buy drinks.

"Don't worry about it," she said, "I have a few bucks." She told me her name was Maggie and I introduced myself.

I asked, "Where are you from?"

"Revelstoke, British Columbia. It's in Canada." We talked until the band took a break.

The lead singer from the band came to our table and asked, "Who is this?"

"He's my friend," she answered.

He just mumbled, "Whatever," and walked off.

Maggie was dating the band's singer, Mark, and had come to watch him perform. I said, "I don't want to cause any problems with Mark." I offered to move back to my table, and she assured me that they were in an open relationship.

"I'm sure he doesn't mind."

I felt dumb but had to ask. "What's an open relationship?"

"We agree to be with whomever we want to as long as we don't leave the other hanging," she explained. "We just make sure each other knows when we will be elsewhere." I guess this was part of the whole sexual revolution thing. I was still like a kid in a candy store, and she was definitely candy.

She ended up leaving with me that evening. I wasn't due back at the halfway house until ten so we headed to her motel room. She was surprised that I wanted to just talk instead of having sex.

She asked, "Are you gay?"

"No way," I said. "I have never met anyone as beautiful and sweet as you and I just don't want to mess it up."

She drove me home, and we talked along the way. She had tons of questions about my past and my crimes. Reluctantly, I shared my life with her. I feared that if she knew me, she wouldn't want to see me again. I thought about that first girl who said she didn't want a relationship, just sex. So I was hesitant to ask if I could see her again. But before I could get up the courage to ask, she did.

"When can you be out tomorrow?"

"I have to be out of the house by 8:00 in order to hunt for a job," I told her.

"Can I pick you up?" she questioned.

"That would be nice." We spent a week searching the want ads, looking for a job I thought I could fit into. I enjoyed hanging out with Maggie.

CHAPTER TWELVE

BECOMING A CITY DWELLER

I showed up at Mr. Smith's office again first thing Monday morning with the *Seattle Times* want ads in my hand. I had circled an ad I wanted to ask him about:

Seattle Bank and Trust
Wanted: Bank Vault Orderly
Experience Required

I told him, "I have experience cleaning out bank vaults."

He just smiled and said, "Don't even think about it."

I ended up applying for a job as a physical therapy aide at Seattle General Hospital. I walked into the interview and shook hands with Gene Fields, the resident physical therapist. "Before I fill out the application," I said, "I don't want to waste your time, and I don't want you to waste mine. I just got out of federal prison for bank robbery. If you have a problem with that, just let me know. If not then, let's proceed."

"Are you on parole?" he asked.

I answered, "Yes."

"I assume they will be keeping good tabs on you, so I shouldn't need to worry. Right?"

I really didn't have a lot to put on the application, so I just talked to him. He hired me.

Maggie went back to Canada but said she would visit again. I started missing her. There were still lots of girls around but she was different. She was interested in me—who I was, and my life.

I really liked working at the hospital. I prepared a lot of hot packs and refilled the lotions bottles. I also performed ultrasound therapy, Medco Sonlator, and Shortwave Diathermy. These were all machines I didn't even know existed when I started, but learned to operate as time went on. Plus, my boss, Gene, would invite me to barbeques at his house almost every weekend.

I was wanting friends and someone I could talk to, but it seemed like sex was all everyone wanted. No relationships, just sex. I began to feel really empty, like I had nothing of value to anyone, and no matter how much I looked for value in others, I was disappointed. At times, it looked like I was living in a world of zombies, like in a movie I had seen in prison a year earlier, *Garden of the Dead*. Just bumping into each other with no real meaning in life. It felt kind of like a lottery ticket. Even though you lose time and time again, you still buy the next ticket thinking, *This one could be it.*

CHAPTER THIRTEEN

THE BITTER END

I never drank for fear of getting busted. But I loved being with people who accepted me for who I was. The Bitter End was a pub at 705 Pike Street in downtown Seattle. Frank James Houchin, Jr. and his wife, Patty, owned and ran it. Frank also played guitar and sang there on Friday and Saturday nights. Frank would always tell the bartender to give me a Coke because he knew I was pretty much broke all the time. The Bitter End became my favorite bar and I was there almost every night until I had to head back to the halfway house.

Frank asked me to bring my guitar in and jam with him on a few songs. He then asked me to fill in for him whenever he wasn't able to be there. No pay, but tips and free drinks all evening. Pretty soon I was playing there almost every weekend.

One evening, I was in the middle of a song when I saw a man grab a woman by the throat as she sat on a bar stool at the counter. The protector in me reared its head. I called out to him "Let her go! Touch her again and we are going to have a problem."

He apologized and backed away from her. About two songs later I watched as he backhanded her across the face. I jumped up and ran over and knocked the crap out of him.

"Get the hell out of here," I said. "You are 86'ed. I don't ever want to see you in here again." The whole bar erupted in cheers. I went back to the stage and continued with the next song.

Pretty soon someone came up to me and asked, "Hey, John, can I get another beer?"

"I'm playing music," I said, "Ask the bartender."

"We can't; you kicked him out."

I put my guitar away and called Patty. She asked me to tend the bar until she and Frank could get there. They weren't mad. In fact, Frank said, "Good job, John. If I were here, I would have done the same thing."

I was sitting near the pool table one evening waiting for the couple playing to finish their game. I always liked it when couples played because they usually finished the game with a few balls left on the table. When two really good guys played, they'd only leave two or three balls.

The couple finished their game and sat down. I grabbed a cue and began shooting around the seven balls they had left. I was setting up a couple of trick shots that a regular customer named Jake had taught me a few days earlier.

A guy walked in the door who I swear looked like Huggy Bear from the TV show *Starsky & Hutch*. He was wearing a white polyester jumpsuit, and sporting a white hat with dingle balls hanging from it. Shiny white shoes and a bright red belt. He started in on me. "Play a game for twenty bucks," he said.

"I'm sorry, I have no money," I answered. Then he really turned it up, once he saw I wasn't going to be a challenge to him.

"How about we play one for fifty?" he asked.

"Like I said, I have no money to play for any amount," I replied as I sat down.

He kept ranting on, and I think people were getting annoyed with him.

About ten minutes later a guy came in selling pool cues. He spread them over the pool table and opened a few of the cases for inspection. I spotted one that was a beaut. It was nineteen ounces and straight as an arrow. Felt good in my hand. The leather case was beautiful. As I was admiring it, a man from the bar walked over and asked me, "Which one of these cues do you like?"

I showed him, and he asked the guy selling them, "How much for this one?"

"$260."

"We'll take it," the guy from the bar said. He then turned to Huggy Bear and said, "He has money now. Put your money where your mouth is. One game for a hundred."

Huggy replied, "We'll play for twenty."

"No, you'll play for the hundred you challenged him to."

They argued a bit, then each handed a C-note to the bartender, which is customary. He hangs on to the wager, then hands it to the winner. I noticed that the man from the bar was dressed in a tuxedo and his wife was dressed to the nines also. Really looked out of place for The Bitter End. He came over to me and asked, "Can you beat this guy?"

"I have no clue. I've never seen him before."

"No worries. Just do your best." Then he sat down.

Huggy Bear racked them up and announced, "We're playing Nine Ball, call every shot, one-handed."

This annoyed me. I had never tried one-handed. I saw no reason for it. But I broke. I sank one ball on the break and only made one more. His turn, he ran the remaining balls, except the nine. When he missed the last shot, he left me nearly frozen on the end rail with the nine frozen on the other end. I decided I wasn't going to win, so I just called the nine, one rail back in the corner pocket. I just let it rip, expecting to lose. It went in.

The whole bar erupted. I was in shock. I walked up to the bar and the bartender handed me the $200. I walked over to the man in the tuxedo to hand it to him.

"No, you keep it," he said. "You earned it."

"But at least keep the cue and the half you put up," I said.

"No. I want you to have it. It's worth it to put a guy like that in his place and see you shut him up." he said with a grin. "Also, give me a call if you ever need someone to back you in a game."

He handed me a bar napkin with a phone number and "B.R." on it. Then he just left. I asked Frank if he knew who the guy was and he said, "I think he once said he was a federal judge."

CHAPTER FOURTEEN

MOVING ON

I had just walked into the halfway house and the gay guy at the front desk took me to the side of the office. "Remember when I saved your ass from going back to prison?"

I said, "Yeah?"

"Time to pay me back," he stated.

"How?" I was hoping he wasn't getting even weirder on me.

"Well, you always roll your own cigarettes and everybody knows it, right?"

"I guess," I replied.

"Well, I have a problem, and you are going to help me out of it."

"How?" I asked

"I was talking to the boss, and I went to shake out a cigarette from my pack of Marlboros. I forgot that I'd stuck a joint in there and it popped out right in front of Mr. Boren."

"What can I do about that?" I asked.

"I told him I traded you a roll-your-own for one of my Marlboros. Now I need you to go into the office and ask a question. Any question. Then pull out one of your homemade cigarettes and ask Boren if he would trade one with you."

"I'm sure he won't," I said.

"It doesn't matter, John. Just offer."

I did as he asked. Don't know what came of it; I never heard. I guess it worked. The gay guy was still there a week later when my time was up.

I was eventually released from the Bishop Lewis house to an apartment I found in the newspaper. However, it was a roach-infested box that seemed even smaller than my cell in prison. No heat and no AC. The bathroom was shared, and near the other end of the building. I hated it. The same evening I moved in, I went out dancing downtown near Pioneer Square with David Morta. He introduced me to a couple of his friends from New York, Peter De La Cruz and Lillian La June. I liked them right off the bat.

Peter said he was Puerto Rican and Lillian was Jewish. They were impressive, great dancers. Peter also had a big white van that said VIP on the side of it. He had bought it from a dry cleaner in New York, but he said VIP stood for Very Important Puerto Rican. The conversation turned to my living situation and without hesitation, they offered for me to move in with them. "We have a two-bedroom apartment," Peter said. "Why don't you just take our other room?"

"It would be a bit before I can chip in anything. I have a new job and won't get paid for another two weeks," I said.

"We aren't worried about it. There is more to life than money."

"Do you think that would be okay with the apartment manager?" I asked.

Lillian said, "Since we are the managers, I think we'll be just fine."

As we were getting to know each other, a guy from prison walked in the door. Danny Whitehead and I weren't friends but we knew of each other. He was a nice guy. I invited him to join us and asked, "How long have you been out?"

"I just got to Bishop Lewis today," he said. "I'm on a 90-minute pass to get shaving gear and a toothbrush."

I told him, "Coincidently, I just got out of there this morning."

He said he knew nothing of Seattle so I offered to show him around. "I am off work Saturday so I can meet you at the halfway house, and we could go get lunch or something."

"That would be great," he replied.

Peter, Lillian, and I left a few minutes later and drove to my apartment to gather my things. I hadn't even unpacked the two boxes I'd moved in with. I was impressed with how nice their apartment was, and felt like my life was making a turn for the better.

The next couple of days were great. I settled in and even went to get my driver's license. Peter let me use his van for the test. On Friday night, Peter, Lillian, Dave, and I went out dancing at a bar called Shelly's Leg near Pioneer Square under the Highway 99 viaduct. Apparently, Shelly worked at the bar and would walk to work. One day she got hit by a train on her way to tend bar. She lost a leg as a result and received a large settlement from the accident. She bought the bar with money she received, remodeled it as a dance club, and renamed it. It was a very popular site. We stayed out until 2:00 A.M. when it closed.

The next morning I was supposed to meet Danny at the halfway house but I was tired, and called to cancel or reschedule.

I called and the gay guy at the front desk answered. He told me Danny had left for the day but then he said, "I am disappointed in you, John."

"Why?" I responded.

"I had high hopes for you, sweetie. But. There is a very attractive *someone* here looking for you. And . . . it's a girl. Damn it."

"Who?" I asked.

"She said her name is Maggie. Or something like that," he said and handed her the phone.

"John?" I heard.

"Maggie?" I asked.

"Yes."

"Hold on." With that, I laid down the phone, grabbed Peter's keys from the table, and ran to the van. I drove the short few blocks to the Bishop Lewis House and parked right in front. I ran through the door and saw she was still holding the phone.

I called out, "Maggie!"

She turned around and saw me. I realized that I had said "Hold on," but neglected to say, "I'll be right there."

"Where are your things?" I asked.

"At the bus station. In a locker."

We drove to the Greyhound station and retrieved her luggage. Then we went to the apartment. As we were unpacking her suitcase, I realized I hadn't asked Peter and Lillian if I could move her in with me. In fact, I hadn't even asked Maggie if she wanted to move in with me. I was really thinking I might be in over my head, looking for something that just wasn't to be.

Lillian and Peter emerged from their bedroom and sat with us at the kitchen table. "Who is this?" Lillian asked.

I introduced them and said, "I suppose I should explain what's going on."

"That would be nice," Peter said.

"You could say I jumped to conclusions about bringing her here, but the truth is, I didn't even think about it. I haven't concluded anything. In fact, I realized just a moment ago that I didn't even ask Maggie if she wanted to be here."

"How long will you be in town? And how long would you want to stay in our house?" Lillian asked.

"I have no idea. I just got off the bus this morning," Maggie responded.

"If you guys want us to go, I understand" I said.

Both Peter and Lillian said, almost in unison, "No way. This is cool."

I then asked Maggie, "Do you think you might want to live with me?"

She said, "Yes."

I asked, "What about Mark?"

"I haven't seen him since the night I met you. He was pissed and didn't come back to the motel."

We took her stuff into the bedroom and started unpacking. She saw the photo of the prison on my wall and asked about it. I told her how it was my higher power to help keep me from going back to prison.

"Sounds pretty smart," she said.

Later that same day, when Peter and Lillian were out, Maggie and I sat down to talk. We decided to define what our relationship would be. We concluded that we would have an open relationship similar to what she had with Mark before. We would be open and honest with each other and always make sure to take care of our needs first. If either of us wanted to see someone else, it would be with prior notice to the other. No sneaking around.

To be honest, I'm not sure if I was playing "go along to get along" or if she was. Perhaps we both thought that was what the other wanted, and we were just trying to be supportive. Either way, it was strange.

We stayed there for a couple of weeks, then Peter told us that the owners of the building had another property that needed managers. "If you want, I can introduce you guys to them."

"That would be great," I said.

We met the owners and they offered us the job. It didn't pay anything except free rent and utilities, unless we had to clean and paint apartments after move outs.

So we moved into Unit Number 1, a furnished apartment at 1517 Boylston Avenue. We were responsible for collecting the rents and keeping the halls and laundry room clean. We did minor repairs and would call plumbers or electricians as needed.

As we moved in, Maggie stuck my prison photo on the wall beside the front door. "I want to make sure you see it whenever you go out," she said.

I thought Maggie was nineteen years old. That's what her ID said. But then she told me she was really seventeen. She applied for and got hired to wait tables at The Alaskan, a bar across the street from The Bitter End.

I was getting restless working at the hospital. I really didn't like putting my hands on people, especially the old people. I decided to look for another job and responded to an ad for a delivery driver at The Copy Company downtown. They hired me and really felt it was a much better fit. I also enjoyed playing my blues harp as I drove around. I didn't like the manager, but the printer was a nice guy. Michael Crumpacker. I thought it was really cool to meet someone with a name as weird as mine, Swanger. We became friends. Maggie and I would go dancing with Michael and his wife, Maria. We also attended several concerts at big venues around Seattle.

Willie Nelson was doing a concert downtown in Seattle at the Paramount Theater, so Maggie and I went, along with Steve Culver. I brought one of my promotional "wanted" posters with me, hoping to get his autograph. I had Waylon Jennings, Kris Kristofferson, Johnny Cash, and Merle Haggard. I just needed Willie to complete the set. As the concert was ending, I walked down the aisle to the stage.

A bouncer said "You can't go to the stage." I ignored him and just walked past him. He grabbed me but fell and I continued on toward the stage dragging him. Steve held the bouncer back as I got to the stage.

Willie said, "Let him go."

I said, "Looking for your autograph, Willie."

He looked at my poster and said, "Lefty, huh? Looks like you're keeping some pretty good company there."

I thanked him for the autograph and as he left the stage he turned back to me. "Good luck with that career, John, a.k.a. Lefty."

CHAPTER FIFTEEN

SETTLING IN

Between my job, Maggie's pay and tips at The Alaskan, and my tips at The Bitter End, we were able to save a few bucks. Especially since we didn't have rent or utilities to pay.

The newly remodeled building was beginning to fill up with tenants. Everyone was busy running around town buying up the latest TVs, VCRs, stereos, BBQ grills, and microwave ovens. We decided to not buy anything on credit. That first month, we bought an Amana Radar Range microwave oven. The next month, we bought a large color TV. Every month, we bought something else and paid cash for it. Within a year we had everything the other tenants had, except for the bills.

We had worked there fewer than three months when we came home one afternoon to find someone had broken into the apartment and stolen all the rent money. We were sure it was someone who lived in the building, because they didn't bother anything else and went right to where the rents were kept.

We called the owners, and then called the police. The officers who responded checked the door and the file box for prints.

One of the officers said, "You should get a small gun for protection."

I responded, "I can't. I'm an ex-con and not allowed to own one."

He asked, "Do you mind if I ask what you were in prison for?"

"Not at all," I told him. "I was convicted in 1971 of bank robbery."

"Wow. You robbed a bank?" he questioned.

"Actually, I robbed a bunch of banks and stores."

As they were leaving, he said, "We will try to check in on you guys every chance we get." I thanked him.

A few days later the officer came back. "First off," he said, "my name is Robert Fleming, but you can call me Bob." He asked if we could go for coffee. "I would like to discuss a few things with you."

I said, "We can put a pot on right here, if you don't mind."

He checked me out, and saw that I was who I said I was. Then he said, "I would like to make a proposition to you."

"What kind of proposition?" I asked.

"I think it would be cool to write a book with you. And then also form a security company to show stores and banks how to decrease their chances of being robbed."

"What would you want from me?" I asked.

"Start writing down anything you can remember about the robberies. How you did them. Your methods. And write the things that would cause you to pick a place to rob, and the things that would cause you to reject a place."

I told him I was busy with my work and playing in the bar, but would do my best.

Bob said, "I'll check in a couple of times a week, and you can give me what you have, and I will give you a few bucks for your time."

"Okay," I said, "but no particulars about specific robberies, just how we pulled them off. Okay?"

"Exactly. How does this sound to you? *Cops & Robbers: How to Guard Your Store from Being Robbed. An Educational Manual Written by an Ex-cop and an Ex-robber.*"

"That sounds great," I answered.

He left, and Maggie said, "I hope he isn't really just looking to change careers."

"I never thought about that. I hope not," I said.

I dug out my journals and started copying things from them. I decided not to give too much on each page I wrote for him, because I wanted to receive as much money as possible. If I told him everything in one sitting there would be no reason to keep coming back.

Bob started coming by twice a week, and each time he would hand me either a fifty or a hundred. I was thinking I would even quit my job at The Copy Company. After all, I was making more than enough between The Bitter End and my new writing gig. Sweet.

I ended up staying with The Copy Company for about five more months before I quit.

CHAPTER SIXTEEN

RECONCILE WITH FAMILY?

Maggie wanted to know everything about my life and especially my family. I think she was saddened by the things I went through as a kid and the things that led me into the life I had chosen. She wanted to meet my family.

"Family is everything," she said. "You need to reconcile with your parents."

I, however, wasn't as keen on the idea. "Why?"

"Because it's the right thing to do," she answered.

I called my parole officer, Mr. Smith, and asked about transferring my parole to Dallas, Texas.

"Are you sure that's what you want to do?" he asked.

"Yes," I answered.

"Give me a couple of days and I'll make it happen," he replied.

By the end of the week we had resigned as apartment managers. Maggie quit at The Alaskan and I told Frank and Patty I was leaving town and couldn't play at the bar any longer. We packed up our things and hit the road.

Three days later, we pulled into the driveway at mom's house. Everyone came to see us and meet Maggie. Both my brothers and both my sisters were there. Walt, my stepfather, was out repossessing cars.

"I have no idea when he will be home," Mom said.

"No worries, Mom," I replied. "I know how it is."

Mom said we could set up our room in a large screened-in porch area that was fairly secluded. It had canvas tarps we could pull down for privacy and open up if it got too hot. Nothing fancy, but we had a place to stay. Once again, Maggie posted my prison photo by the door.

Within a day I was repossessing cars with Walt. He promised me he would give me $40 per car. I thought, *Between that and free rent we will be okay.* Maggie even went with me sometimes on repos. I think she enjoyed the adrenaline rush.

I called Garry Smith and asked about meeting up with my new parole officer.

"I'll set something up soon," he said. "But in the meantime, don't worry about it. Just keep sending your monthly reports to me like always."

A couple of weeks later I was out with Walt picking up cars. We stopped for lunch.

"Tell me how you managed to get away with so many robberies for so long," he asked.

I told him how we always hid in the trunk of the second car after ditching the stolen car we used in the robbery.

He said, "Shoot, John. We could pull off that kind of thing right here."

We ended up planning out a robbery of a grocery store near where my grandmother Nanny lived.

Walt said, "You can flee on foot around the building. Then climb into the trunk of a car I'll have hooked up on the wrecker. They'll never think of checking for you there."

The next day Walt bought a wig and a fake moustache and dug up an old cowboy hat from somewhere, and I got ready. We were set to go. We drove to the venue, and Walt handed me his pistol. I was about to get out of the car when I saw a police car drive by.

"It's clear," Walt said. "He's gone."

I just couldn't do it. My nerves started going crazy, just like in the old days. I thought, *I can't go through all this again.* "Walt, I can't do it," I said.

He responded, "I understand. You lost your nerve."

I couldn't say if Walt was being compassionate or if he was being condescending. Probably the latter. But I realized that after all these years I was still trying to please him. I also realized that I was still disposable to Walt, and I needed to get away from him. Probably forever.

As soon as we got back to the house, I called Garry Smith. "Garry, I want to come back to Seattle. Sorry to be jerking you around with this, but it's what we really need to do," I said.

Garry said, "I know you do, John. That's why I have you marked as visiting relatives out of district. I never transferred you."

"Really?" I asked incredulously..

"You don't belong there, John," he answered.

Walt never paid me anything. We told my mom we needed to go back to Seattle. She gave us $500 she had saved up and kept in a coffee can in the laundry room. We also had the money we left Seattle with. Somewhere around $800.

Three days later we were in Seattle. We stayed with Peter and Lillian for almost two weeks until we found another gig as apartment managers.

CHAPTER SEVENTEEN

THE ST. REGIS HOTEL

"If you want it to float, it's going to take a little longer."
George Todd

We moved in to the Belvedere Apartments, a three-story triangular building with eight apartments on each floor. It was only a few blocks from where we were before. As we were moving in, Maggie called me into the living room, saying, "I have a gift for you."

"What?" I asked.

She opened a bag and pulled out my prison photo, but she had framed it and put in a strip of paper across the bottom that said:

> *"We are programmed to receive.*
> *You can check out any time you like,*
> *But you can never leave!"*
> "Hotel California," The Eagles © 1976

Again she hung it by the front door.

We unpacked. That week we once again started the process of acquiring all the necessities: TV, VCR, stereo, and microwave. Unlike Boylston, this apartment wasn't furnished. So first the basic needs: coffee pot, bed, and kitchen table and chairs. We hit a ton of garage sales and flea markets.

I found a job right away at the St. Regis Hotel. The owner had a hotel, a restaurant, and a bar, all in that location, and a yacht yard in West Seattle.

They hired me to walk around downtown and refill the vending machines. I was responsible for keeping them clean and trying to fix them if they broke, and for reporting problems to the owner if it was something I couldn't fix. He taught me a lot about vending and showed me into the basement of the hotel where he had several dozen broken and cannibalized machines. He said I could take any parts I needed to keep the route running smoothly.

The owner's name was George Todd. I thought he was the smartest man I'd ever known. He told me he and several friends got out of the Navy at the same time, pooled their severance pay to build a yacht, and then they sailed around the world in it. Once back in Seattle, they sold it and split up the money. George took his share and built a bigger and better yacht. He sold it and bought the hotel.

He then opened a yacht company where he built three or four yachts each year. He also bought XKE Jaguars from rich Hollywood types who grew tired of their expensive toys and sold them cheap. He would usually pay around five thousand for one, install a Cobra V8 engine in it, and sell it for about twenty thousand. Everything he did made money.

It wasn't long before the person who made the sandwiches for the vending route quit, and I was put into that job also. Then the morning cook at The Marketplace started showing up late, and I had to start getting there early in the mornings to cover for her. Next thing you know, I was virtually running the restaurant. Minimum wage was $2.30 an hour. I was making $5.50 an hour, but I was running myself ragged.

One day I walked into George's office. I noticed he had a drafting table with some plans for a yacht on it. I asked him, "How long does it take to build a yacht?"

"Well, that depends," he replied. "If I take six months to design it, it'll take two years to build. But if I take two years to design it, it'll only take six months to build." Then after a chuckle, he added, "Of course, if you want it to float, it's going to take a bit longer."

George asked, "When are you going to make an honest woman of the girl you live with?"

"What do you mean?" I asked.

"You need to marry her, John," he answered.

That evening I began to feel concerned that Maggie would go back to Canada again, like she did before I got out of Bishop Lewis. "Maggie, we need to get married," I told her.

"Why?" she asked.

"It's the right thing to do," I answered.

That evening Maggie met a drunk customer at The Alaskan who told her that her cheating fiancé was leaving town with someone else, and asked Maggie for a ride home. When I picked up Maggie from work that evening, we drove the lady to her apartment. She invited us in and brewed a pot of coffee. The lady said, "You two obviously belong together. I can tell you are in love."

We drank coffee and tried to sober her up. A half hour later she said she was going to bed. As we walked out the door, she took off her rings and handed them to Maggie. "Here," she said, "you need these. I have no use for them." Then she removed her watch and gave it to her also.

On the way home Maggie said, "Yes."

"Yes what?" I asked.

"Yes, I'll marry you," she answered.

CHAPTER EIGHTEEN

A VISIT TO THE J.P.

April 16, 1976

George Todd did the entire wedding plan and also provided the catering and all the extras. The reception was at the home of the hotel manager, Masamu (Matsu) Kindo.

But first, Maggie and I headed to the justice of the peace's house along with Frank and Patty as witnesses. It was a simple wedding. No vows and no pomp and circumstance. A simple "I do" on both parts and, poof, we were married.

Was I really in love? Maggie was my first-ever real girlfriend. I think perhaps I just didn't ever want to lose her. She was someone who actually cared for me, and didn't judge me.

The honeymoon consisted of a night at the St. Regis and then back to work in the morning. However, they did allow me to come in late.

We headed home to find flowers on our doorstep from my older sister, Evelyn. I wasn't sure how she knew I was getting married, but she did. We received gifts from several of the people who worked at the hotel, and as well one from The Bitter End. The apartment owners bought us a blender, a toaster, and a basket of fruit.

We spent the next few days making the necessary changes to our life. First Maggie headed up to British Columbia to change her driver's license to Swanger. She left her fake ID at home. Then she filled out the necessary papers to change her Canadian Social Insurance card to Swanger also. We amended our contract with the apartment owners to reflect her new name, and we changed the name on our bank account and her Seattle library card.

Garry Smith called me into his office, and I told him I got married.

He said, "Legally, you are supposed to get my approval first. At the very least, you should have told me you were planning on it."

I said, "I'm sorry, Mr. Smith. Am I in trouble?"

"No," he said. "I just wanted to give you a hard time." Then he added, "Honestly, if you wouldn't have married that girl, I would have been disappointed."

A year later things were getting tough at the hotel. A couple of workers quit, and I ended up becoming the unofficial manager of the restaurant. I was responsible for managing but wasn't making more money.

George called me to his office and said, "I got you and Maggie an anniversary gift." He handed me two tickets to the very first game of the new Seattle Mariners. On April 6, 1977, in front of a sold-out crowd of 57,762 at the Kingdome, they lost 7–0 to the Angels.

I soon got to the point where I felt like I needed to quit working there. I've never been the type who could just walk in and say, "I quit." I decided to go in and demand a raise. That way, when they said no I would feel more justified in quitting.

I told Matsu I needed to talk to George.

He said, "I was just coming to get you, because George wants to talk to you."

I waited outside George's office on the top floor trying to decide how much I should ask for. I wanted to make sure it was large enough so they would say no. Finally they called me in. Matsu, George and his business partner, Walter, were there.

"John," George said, "you are doing a great job and I want you to know how pleased we are that you are part of the St. Regis family. However since you are the de facto manager of the restaurant, we feel you need to start looking more professional. You need to dress appropriately. No more jeans, and you need to start wearing a button-down shirt. Every day. Look sharp, John"

My blood began to boil. I was pissed. I didn't even have the money to buy enough food, much less fancy clothes. I thought, *This is going to be easier than I thought.*

I said, "George, I can't afford nice clothes. Everything I owned was purchased at the Goodwill. If you guys want me to dress better, cut me a check, and I'll be happy to go out and buy them.

"Also, I want to say while I'm in here that I want a raise. I want eight dollars an hour, starting with the beginning of this pay period. And lastly, I no longer want to answer to Matsu. I want to work directly for you, George."

George said angrily, "John, you realize you are going about this the wrong way. You can't walk in here and start demanding anything."

"However, this is the way it is going," I said. He told me to wait out in the hall while they discussed it.

As I sat there I thought, *There. That should do it.* Finally, Matsu stuck his head out the door and invited me in. I walked in thinking I was for sure going home early.

George handed me a check. I thought it was my final paycheck until I looked at it. It was noted, "clothing allowance." And it was for eight hundred dollars.

George said, "Effective the beginning of this month you are making eight dollars an hour, and, from now on, you work for me. Not Matsu. Take the rest of today off, and tomorrow. Go buy some clothes."

That weekend, Willie Nelson was back in town. This time he was at the Seattle Center Coliseum. We managed to get seats near the front, and after the concert started, we made our way up to just in front of the stage. We were actually standing right in front of Willie. As he finished the first song, *Whiskey River,* he turned to look at me. "How's that career going, Lefty?" he asked. "Or, it's John, isn't it?"

I smiled and said, "Great." He then handed me his guitar pick and grabbed another from his mic stand. I was in heaven.

After the concert we headed to the West Veranda, a country bar and dance hall. We were watching our favorite local band, Stampede Pass, when Bee Speers, Willie's bass player, stuck his head in the door. He immediately backed out and closed the door. Then Willie and his whole band walked in. A few minutes later they were invited to the stage and they played for about an hour. We were shocked. Between him remembering my name from more than a year ago, and now this free concert, Willie became my hero.

CHAPTER NINETEEN

WITNESS DEFECTION

Two weeks later George called me back into his office. "Your parole officer called, he said. "He needs to see you right away."

"Did he say what it was about?" I asked.

"No, he just wanted me to know so I could let you take off a couple of hours, I guess," he replied.

I hopped on the bus and headed to the federal building. I was apprehensive even though I had done nothing wrong. My anxiety was building. As I walked into Mr. Smith's office, I was greeted by two federal marshalls.

One of them said, "Turn around and put your hands behind your back."

I did, but asked, "What's going on?"

After I was handcuffed the other marshall handed some papers to Garry. Then he said to me, "You are due in court in Los Angeles in a few hours."

"For what?" I asked.

"They will let you know as soon as you arrive in L.A." he answered.

With that, they took me to SeaTac Airport, uncuffed me, and escorted me to the gate. I could see them waiting in the boarding area until the plane began to taxi toward the runway.

The flight was nerve-racking. I was a wreck by the time we landed. I walked off the plane, and met a marshall holding a sign that read, SWANGER.

He told me, "You are here to testify in a trial."

"What trial?" I asked.

He told me the name, but I didn't recognize it. He drove me to an office building where I was to meet with the prosecutor. As I walked into the office waiting area, I saw David Brinkerhoff (a guy I knew from prison) and several other inmates.

"What's going on?" I asked Brinkerhoff.

"It's the trial for the Hernandez stabbing," he answered.

I waited as, one by one, they each were called into the prosecutor's office. Finally I was called in.

The prosecuting attorney said, "We have it on good knowledge that you were not only present at the assault but witnessed it firsthand. Up close and personal."

The fear I had been experiencing all morning, the stress of the flight, and not knowing what was happening had put me on high alert. In the back of my mind, I felt there was always the possibility of going back to prison. So I certainly didn't want to do anything that might put a target on my back, should I ever get sent back. I remembered the prison code: you don't ever snitch or testify against anyone.

The prosecutor laid a sheet of paper in front of me with six pictures of black men on it. "Tell me which one of these, if any, you recognize. And if you do, tell me how you know them."

I knew most of them from prison. The center one at the bottom, number five, was the guy who had stabbed Hernandez. I looked over the page for a few seconds, looked up at him, and then looked back at the photos. I said, "I can't tell. To me, those people all look kind of the same."

He said, "Take your time."

I pointed at number three, and said "I guess it could be him." Then I pointed at number one and said, "Or even him. But I'm not sure." The prosecutor sent me back into the lobby and called for the marshall, who told me to follow him.

I asked, "Are we heading to the airport?"

He said, "No I'm taking you to your hotel. First, we'll stop and pick up some toiletries and a lunch." We stopped by a sub shop and then he handed me two twenties and a ten, saying, "This should hold you for the duration of your stay."

Then, as he checked me into the hotel, he said, "Be ready. I'll pick you up at 8:00 A.M. sharp."

Morning came and I was still not willing to testify. I felt like I needed to convince them that I wanted to but had nothing to offer. Once again, I was taken to the prosecutor's office. There, another attorney ran me through the questions. Then he showed me the page with the floor layout of K-Unit, which I had signed while I was still in prison, showing where I was during the stabbing. At the time, I'd claimed I was too far away from the stabbing to see anything. He said, "We know you weren't sitting where you said you were."

Then he pulled out another layout. On this one, the exact seat I had been sitting in was marked with my name. Obviously someone, probably Brinkerhoff, had told them where I was during the assault. "That's right, sir," I said, "It's true I was sitting there, but I was so scared that I put my head down and cried. By the time I looked up, it was over and we were getting locked down. I want to help. Tell me which one it is, and I'll identify him. I just really can't tell."

He sent me back into the lobby, then the marshall picked me up again and we headed out.

I asked, "Now are we heading to the airport?"

"Not yet," he said, "we have one more stop to make."

He took me to another office building where I sat in the lobby with several other inmates I knew from prison. These men, however, were all black. I was called into the office and a man introduced himself as Mr. Brighten, lead attorney for the defendant, Grover P. White.

He said, "The prosecutor tells me he doesn't need you to testify. That's good. I was wondering if you might be of use to us. The other side." With that, he handed me the exact same photo line-up as the prosecutor had and asked, "Do you recognize the assailant?"

I was thinking, *While code says don't testify* against *anyone, I damn sure don't want to testify* for *the jerk. Not only was Hernandez a great guy, he was my friend.* So I picked up the sheet of paper and pointed right at number five. "That's him right there. Do you want me to get on the stand and point him out in court? I will if you want me to. Just tell me what you want."

The attorney dismissed me and the marshall took me away again. "We missed the last flight to Seattle," he said, "so you get to enjoy one more night in this, the beautiful City of Angels."

As he dropped me at the hotel I asked what I needed to do next. He said, "Enjoy your evening, but don't drink any alcohol. See a movie or go get dinner. I'll pick you up about 10:30 A.M. and we'll head to LAX."

The next morning I actually enjoyed the flight back to Seattle. I stopped by Garry's office and then headed to work at the St. Regis.

CHAPTER TWENTY

FATE SOMETIMES GIVES YOU WHAT YOU WANT

I walked into the hotel and headed to the time clock. My time card was missing. Matsu walked by. He looked like he was surprised to see me. "George wants to see you immediately," he said. I went upstairs and knocked on the office door.

George called out, "Come in."

I walked in, and George said, "Don't bother sitting down."

"What's going on, George?"

"I'm sorry, John, but we are going to have to let you go. You were given a morning to meet with your parole officer, but you show up for work three days later?"

I told him what happened and said, "It was out of my control."

He simply said, "You should have called."

I realized that if I debated with him he might decide to keep me on. So I shut up. He handed me a final paycheck but deducted four hundred of the eight hundred clothing allowance. He said, "Consider it a gift."

I left and headed back to Garry's office to let him know I lost my job. It was mandatory to immediately report any change of address, employment status, or arrests.

I told Garry and he said, "You know he's right. You should have called him."

I said, "I know. But honestly, that was the last thing on my mind. It never even occurred to me. I'll find another job. Don't worry."

He said, "I have faith in you, John. I'm not worried at all." I told him Maggie was from Canada and her father wanted to meet me. "Is it possible to get a permit to travel to Revelstoke, British Columbia, for a few days?"

He replied, "Canada is out of the jurisdiction of the federal government of the United States. We cannot authorize travel to anywhere we can't retrieve you from. So, no, I can't issue you a permit to travel there. But you have a nice time and call me when you get back."

That evening the owners of the apartments told us they would keep an eye on the place, and, since all the rents had been collected for the month, we were free to go. Maggie told the bar she wouldn't be in for a few days, and we headed out for the four-hundred mile trip. Or perhaps I should say, 675 kilometers?

We pulled into Maggie's father's house about nine in the morning. Richard was an amazing man. He was a retired veteran of the Royal Canadian Air Force, as well as retired from the Canadian Forestry Service. He owned a large house where he ran an automobile junkyard. On the side, he played a 120-year-old banjo mandolin and often played at the local Canadian Legion.

Maggie's family was large—four stepsisters on her dad's side, and two stepbrothers on her mom's. Together Dick and Bernadette had had Marguerite (Maggie) and her younger brother, Bjorne.

We enjoyed hanging out, and I loved getting to know Dick and Bernadette and Bjorne. The rest of their kids were scattered all over western Canada.

Then we packed our bags and headed back to Seattle. At the border, Maggie was denied entry into the US. We showed them our marriage license, but they said that was irrelevant. "You, sir, head on south," the immigration officer said. "And you, ma'am, turn around and head north."

Maggie called out as she walked away, "I'm going for lunch."

We had just left the KFC in White Rock, British Columbia, ten minutes earlier so I drove to Blaine, Washington, and found a phone. I called the KFC and they put her on the phone.

She said, "Where are you?"

"I am at the Shell station in Blaine."

"Just wait there," she said. "I'll be there as soon as I can."

I got back in the car and just tried to sleep. The time in Canada had been refreshing but overall the past couple of weeks had been stressful and exhausting. I lay there for about three hours. Finally I dozed off and was awakened by Maggie tapping on the window. She had hitchhiked back across the border with some students. The border patrol didn't even question her.

We were tired from the trip so we just headed to Birch Bay to spend the night. I was excited to get back to Seattle. I wanted to find another job as soon as possible.

CHAPTER TWENTY-ONE

FINDING OTHER TALENTS

"I'm your boogie man"
KC and the Sunshine Band © 1976

I went to a bar on the north side of Seattle to apply for a job I saw listed in the newspaper: "Bouncer. Must be big and tough. Must have a good disposition and able to defuse any situation." I knew I was tough, and I knew nothing scared me, so I thought, *Why not?*

The manager called me into his office. "Why should I hire you as my bouncer?" he asked.

I said, "Well, I can kick your ass."

The manager reached under the desk and pushed a button. A really large man with tattoos walked in the door. The manager looked up at him, then at me. "What about him?"

"I can kick his ass also."

The big guy looked at me, a bit confused, but saw he had best think twice before making a move.

The manager said, "You know what? I believe you probably could. But the deal is, if I hire you, you would have to whip everyone who causes any problems here. With a big guy like him, he tells them to leave and they do."

He said, "You just aren't as big as I need you to be. Sorry. I wish you were."

He gave me his business card and wrote on the back, "Free drinks for the evening." I went back out to the table where Maggie was sitting, and we ordered drinks. This place was advertised as a strip bar. But there were actually guys dancing on stage. It was weird.

A guy named Levi came over to me and introduced himself to me and Maggie. He said he had met me in the halfway house, but I didn't remember him. He was dancing there.

He said, "Tonight is men's amateur night. It's a strip contest. We dance and the ladies tip us. You keep all the tips you make and then the judges vote. First place gets $100, second $30, and third $20. You know, you are built pretty good, can you dance?"

I told him, "Yes, I can."

He told me he had an extra G-string he would sell to me for five dollars so I could enter the contest. I asked, "Is it new?"

"Still in the package."

I danced that night and won first place. I also made about $80 in tips. Levi said there were different contests in other bars around town. One each night of the week, except for Sunday.

He said, "If you want to meet up tomorrow evening, we can ride together."

In all there were five bars in Seattle with contests, and one on Saturday in Yakima, called The Corral. That first week I danced in all six contests, and took three firsts, two seconds, and a third. Tips and all, I made nearly $700. Levi said it was beginner's luck. "Don't quit your day job, because it changes every week. They just love you because you're new."

The truth is, Levi never finished better than me in a contest. I got tired of traveling to Yakima every Saturday though, so I just danced Monday through Friday and would skip The Corral.

Maggie quit working at The Alaskan and we would play pool most Saturdays at The Bitter End. We would often go to dinner with Frank and Patty, who showed us some fancy restaurants. Frank always insisted on paying for dinner. Even at the Terry Avenue Freight House, the most expensive restaurant in Seattle, as far as I knew. Sometimes we would go to dinner before going to The Bitter End. Frank and Patty worked the bar while I played my guitar.

One evening I was taking a break between sets, and walked out of the bar and around the corner to buy a pack of cigarettes. As I walked past the business next door, I saw Frank kissing Maggie in the alcove. He jumped as I walked by and ran back into the bar. When I came back, he asked me to come outside with him, away from Patty.

"John," he said, "I want to apologize for what you saw. I didn't mean to. It just happened."

I said, "Don't worry about it. Maggie and I have an agreement. It's all good."

He said, "Please don't tell Patty." He kept apologizing. I guess he didn't understand. The next week he asked me to lunch and again said he was sorry. He also said he wanted to start paying me $35 a night for playing at the bar.

I don't know if he thought I was worth the money or if he just felt guilty about Maggie. So Steve Culver and I played The Bitter End or at Gibson House almost every weekend.

Not having a day job meant I could spend more time at the bar. I still didn't drink but I loved playing pool. There was an old guy named Jake who was always there. He was about 90 years old and had cataracts in both eyes. Even so, he was perhaps the best pool player I had ever met. He said he used to own a pool hall in Pennsylvania and his son grew up with Willie Mosconi, the world champion straight pool player. He said his son and Willie played pool every evening at his billiards parlor. Every time I came in, he would talk about Willie Mosconi. There were times I thought he was just stringing a line of BS because, after all . . . Willie Mosconi?

One afternoon I came in, and Jake said, "Willie is in town."

"Really?"

"Yeah and he's going to come in and have a drink. I told him about you and he asked that you join us."

Still not sure if Jake was serious or not, I said, "Sure."

Jake said, "Do me a favor and don't make a big deal about it being Willie Mosconi." I was thinking like a pool hustler and thought he wanted to make a few bucks.

But Jake said, "No, he just wants to enjoy the evening without having to sign autographs or do trick shots."

About an hour later, Willie walked in, wearing a pinstripe suit. He was much younger than Jake but still he was in his sixties. He sat down, and Jake introduced us. Right away, Willie started talking to me about pool and telling me about table management. "The easiest shot to make is the straight-in shot. If you can make every shot a straight-in shot, then you can win every game."

He added, "You always need to play position. Watch where you put the cue ball. Make it land where you want it to, and you'll have easy shots all night."

About a half hour into his visit, he said, "Let me show you a few things." We racked the balls, and he broke. He started making shots, and after each shot he was, indeed, lined up for the next shot. Soon a guy at the bar walked over and asked if he could play the winner.

Jake said, "We aren't really playing. Just fooling around."

The guy said, "Would you be interested in playing a game of eight-ball for a hundred?"

Willie said, "If you insist."

The man and Willie each handed Frank a C-note. Willie racked the balls and told the man he could have the break. The man broke and made the six on the break and proceeded to run out four other balls. Then he missed.

Willie took a cue and began methodically pocketing his stripes. All seven of them. He was down to the eight ball and had it straight in from only about 18 inches. He lined up the shot and called "Eight-ball corner pocket." Then he flipped the cue around and held it more like a big pencil resting on his shoulder. "Four rails off your three ball," he said.

He popped it, and the eight ball hit both rails at the corner pocket then traveled to both rails at the opposite corner. Then it traveled back, tapped the three ball that was resting on the rail near the pocket, and dropped in.

Everyone was applauding. The guy walked to the bar, and Frank handed him the two hundred. He in turn handed it to Willie. "You're pretty good," he said. "Don't get me wrong, you're no Willie Mosconi, but you are pretty good."

I tried not to laugh. Jake couldn't help it, though. Almost a belly laugh.

Seattle passed a regulation that said if you owned a bar and served alcohol to someone who was drunk and they got in an accident, you could be liable for any damage they do. And if they killed or injured someone, you could even be arrested.

This brought about a meeting with Frank announcing to the entire staff, including me, that under no circumstances were we to allow anyone who was drunk to be served. "In fact, if you even think they are anywhere near drunk, ask them to leave," Frank said.

I was playing and singing on a Saturday evening and stood up to take a break. I walked to the bar and ordered a Coke. On my way back to the stage, I saw an obviously drunk man staggering in the front door. I stopped him at the door and said, "I'm sorry, sir, but you are drunk. You can't come in here."

He mumbled something, turned around, and left. I walked to the back and, as I was about to step onto the stage, the same man was entering through the side door. I said, "Sir, I told you that you can't come in here."

"What?" he answered, "Do you own every damn bar in town?"

Life in the big city. I loved it.

CHAPTER TWENTY-TWO

AT 2.5 OF MY 6

All in all, we visited Canada three times during the first half of my third year on parole. We planned to visit more during the remaining three and a half years.

We were well settled into our life as apartment managers. I was still dancing four to five nights a week, and playing on Saturdays and sometimes on Friday as well. Maggie had started dancing also. The same group that led the men's amateur contests began promoting a ladies contest on different nights at the same bars.

Between dancing and playing at The Bitter End and Gibson House, we were making a decent living. I had also started playing during the day at Pike Place Market in downtown Seattle and at several street fairs around town, like the Freemont District Street Festival, the Ballard Street Fair, and the Wallingford Street Fair. During this time, I sometimes ran across a Seattle legend named Baby Gramps. A few times, he invited me to join him playing at the market. He played an old dobro and a kazoo. I would join in with my blues harp and guitar.

One day as I was heading to Pike Place Market, I was transferring busses and saw Garry Smith getting off the bus that I was getting on. I handed him my monthly report. After all, it saved me a stamp. Two weeks later I got a letter from the federal parole office that said, *"You are in violation of the terms of your parole, and are subject to re-incarceration."*

It instructed me to report immediately to my parole officer, so I headed to Mr. Smith's office. He said, "Not a big deal, John. That is just a form letter that is automatically generated when someone neglects to file their monthly report."

"I gave you my report when you were getting off the bus a couple of weeks ago," I replied.

"Either way, I don't have it, so could you please just fill out another while you are here?" he said.

I looked around the office and noticed his grey tweed jacket hanging on the coat rack in the corner. "In fact," I said, "that was the jacket you were wearing when I handed you my report. You stuffed it into the left inside pocket."

Garry stood up, walked to the coat rack, and looked into the pocket. He pulled out the report and smiled. "I am so sorry, John. My fault, not yours. I am going to make this right. It isn't enough just to show that you have the report in. I am going to notify the records department to remove the initial notification that said you were delinquent."

A month later I came home to find a note on our apartment door. It was handwritten, and from Garry:

May 23, 1978
"Bad news, John. You won't have me to kick around anymore.
Please stop by the office so we can finalize this thing."

I freaked out. My brain started cycling with the fear of getting violated and thoughts of prison. I was almost in tears when I walked into Garry's office.

"You okay, John?" he asked.

"I'm freaking out. I haven't done anything wrong. Why am I being violated?"

"I guess my sarcasm got lost in the delivery. You are not being violated. Just the opposite. We are terminating your parole supervision. You are free from further hold of any type. In fact, you could go to Canada anytime you want. Even move there if you wish."

At this point I really began to cry. All the pent-up emotion of the past seven years started to flow.

Garry said, "You should be proud, John. You have been a model prisoner and parolee. I just need you to sign a few forms, and you are free to go."

I thanked him for being a good parole officer. And left.

I went home and told Maggie,

"What do we do now?" she asked.

I said, "Let's move to Canada."

We spent the rest of the day having a garage sale, trying to get rid of all of our things. We ended up giving most of it away to friends and to other tenants of the building. Dave Morta came by and took our microwave and TV. Peter and Lillian took most of the furniture and dishes.

We called the building owners and told them we had to move. We told them Maggie couldn't remain in the U.S., so we had to go to Canada. They were understanding. "When do you need to go?" they asked.

I told them, "We need to leave today." They said they would be right over. Once they arrived, we offered them the remaining furniture, lamps, fans, and linens.

"We can use everything at our other buildings that we rent as furnished."

I felt the need to apologize. "I am sorry to leave you without a manager and with no notice at all."

"Don't worry," they assured us. "We can move another couple in from a different property."

That evening Maggie and I had a big "Getting Off Parole" party. We invited all our friends, including Frank and Patty, Peter and Lillian, David Morta, and Steve Culver and his girlfriend, Connie. We also invited Michael and Maria Crumpacker from the Copy Company. We even invited Matsu and George Todd. Matsu showed up but George didn't. I made my famous guacamole and we had tacos.

Then we packed all we could into our 1962 Thunderbird and headed for the border.

CHAPTER TWENTY-THREE

HEADING FOR THE BORDER

We pulled into Revelstoke and Maggie called her dad. "Would it be okay if we come stay there until we can get a place of our own?" she asked.

Dick told her to come and see what he had just set up. He had no idea we were moving or that I had even gotten off parole. Even so, he was welcoming us with open arms. When we got there he was excited to show us the house trailer he had purchased and set up on the front of his property.

He said, "I had you two in mind when I came across this deal. Your brothers and sisters are always visiting and take up the extra room in the house. I also figured someday you guys would be coming, and I wanted to have a place where you could put your roots back down."

We began unloading the car and setting up our new home.

Dick called us to the house and poured some coffee. I poured some cream into my cup and asked, "Do you take cream, Mr. Storbo?"

"Surely do. And call me Dick, please," he answered. I passed him the cream and grabbed a couple of the biscuits from the plate he had set in front of me. As he pushed the butter dish and jam my way, he said, "I was wondering what your plans are—if, in fact, you have any yet."

I said, "First thing, we need to find work."

"I have a situation you might be able to help me with," he said. "My son-in-law and my eldest daughter, Lenora, live across the road. He has been running the wrecking yard for me but it's a mess and everything is going to pot. Haven't made any money in months. I was wondering if you might be interested in taking over and helping me salvage this salvage yard," he said with a chuckle.

I answered, "I would love to, but I have to tell you I know nothing about running a junk yard. I repossessed cars with my stepfather. I can change oil and minor repairs but not sure what to do after that."

Dick said, "Not to worry. Anything beyond that I can show you as we go."

Not bothering to ask what it paid, I simply said, "It's a deal."

With that he added, "I'll pay you $350 a week. And not any of that funny money from you Yanks either. This will be some of these crisp, colorful, Canadian notes."

"How much for pitching our camp in your second home up front?" I asked.

"I wouldn't dream of booking you anything for that. Simply having my baby girl back around is payment enough," he said. Bjorne came in from his chores and joined us at the table. Just a couple of years younger than Maggie, he had Down syndrome and was a nice kid—and really smart. Dick asked Bjorne if he wanted a sandwich.

"Yes, please," Bjorne answered. "Meat and cheese, please."

Dick started to get up when Maggie intervened. "I'll get it for him. I've missed my little buddy," she said.

Early the next morning, I started moving cars around the lot, trying to create some order within the mess. I cleaned out the rather large barn/shop and started stacking alternators in one area, starters in another, and then batteries, fuel pumps, carburetors, and distributors.

I looked over the wrecked cars and talked to Dick about fixing a few up to sell. He started teaching me to rebuild engines. I rebuilt several Dodge V8s and a Chrysler Slant Six.

We started selling some of the better cars, and Dick and I went to a few auctions throughout B.C., looking for cars to fill the holes in our inventory.

Maggie had found a free Afghan hound in the local paper and brought it home, first dog I'd had since I was a kid, and she was a great dog. She was housebroken and ate leftovers. Easy on the wallet.

CHAPTER TWENTY-FOUR

GETTING DISCOVERED

My cousin, David Wells, came to visit us, and we made up a bed for him in the extra bedroom of the trailer. On Fridays and Saturdays, Maggie, David, and I would go to the local neighborhood tavern called The Big Eddy Pub. We played pool there and would often have dinner. They had great fish and chips.

The Big Eddy always had live music. Bands would come in on Sundays and set up, and then play Monday through Saturday. I thought it was strange that bars could stay open until two A.M. every night of the week except Saturday, when they would have to close by midnight.

It always amazed me how the bands that would come through seemed to hate what they did. They ignored the audience and often even turned their backs on the crowd. It was like they didn't want to be there. I thought, *How can the crowd have a good time if the band is miserable?* They often wouldn't even talk to the audience. Just played their songs and left. *If I ever get to play live again,* I told myself, *I'm going to see that everyone enjoys being there. I'm going to have fun so they will also.*

One Wednesday evening, David, Maggie, and I were at The Big Eddy, listening to a man singing and playing guitar. As he took a break, he came to our table. "You're a musician, aren't you?" he asked.

"Yes, how did you know?" I asked with surprise.

He answered, "By the way you watched my hands instead of my singing."

I said, "That's true. I never thought about it."

"Would you like to play a song?" he asked.

I said, "You bet."

He said, "You're right-handed, aren't you?"

I answered "Nope. I'm a lefty. But that's okay. I'll fumble through."

I got up on stage and turned his right handed guitar over, then stepped up to the microphone and played a Waylon Jennings song, "Good-Hearted Woman."

During the song I could see that the guy was on the pay phone. When I finished he called me to the phone. He said, "Here, talk to your agent."

The lady on the phone introduced herself as Vicki Ballard and said she was in Calgary Alberta, which was 400 km (about 250 miles) away. "Could you come see me Monday to iron out some paperwork before hitting the road?" she asked.

"I suppose I could," I said. "What paperwork?"

"A managerial contract. I will book you to play throughout B.C. and Alberta, and you agree to give me 10% of whatever each booking contract pays."

I got off the phone and headed back to the table. The singer introduced himself to me. "I'm Eddie Dolan. I'm Eddie Dolan, from Kelowna."

I introduced myself, Maggie, and David. "This all sounds great," I told him, "I have a guitar and a large amp. But I don't have a PA system like you have up there. I don't see how I could do this."

He told me he had taken his PA system to the shop the day before for repairs and bought the one on stage to help him get by until the other one was fixed. "I'm here through Saturday night. Come by at closing time and you can take this one. You can pay me $350 for it after you have a few gigs under your belt." I thanked him and we left.

Once home, David asked, "John, do you have enough songs to make it through an entire night of playing?"

"I probably have twenty-five to thirty songs. A few Waylon and Willie, but mostly Merle Haggard and Hank Williams. A few of The Eagles and some Credence Clearwater Revival."

He said, "I think we need to get to work, then." He reached into his bag and pulled out a stack of cassettes, mostly Waylon Jennings a couple of Willie Nelson's and a few others. I had been playing their music for a couple of years in Seattle, but only knew about five song collectively. By all means, "Good Hearted Woman" was my favorite.

David stuck a cassette into Maggie's tape deck. We grabbed paper and pens and started to take down lyrics. We went through all his cassettes and came up with another eighteen songs that I loved and thought I could learn:

Waylon: *This Time, Pick up the Tempo, Bob Wills Is Still the King, Are You Sure Hank Done It This Way? My Heroes Have Always Been Cowboys, Can't You See? I've Always Been Crazy, Ladies Love Outlaws, Rainy Day Woman, A Couple More Years*

Willie: *Shotgun Willie, Blue Eyes Crying in the Rain, Hands on the Wheel, Me and Paul, Mammas Don't Let Your Babies Grow Up to Be Cowboys, Till I Gain Control Again*

Charlie Daniels: *Take This Job and Shove It*

Tompall Glaser: *Put Another Log on The Fire*

I practiced through the night with David helping me memorize the words. The next day we did it again and again. David was working hard to help me get ready. Then he asked, "Do you have anything you have written yourself?"

"Nothing I have put to music," I answered. We spent the next couple of hours writing what would end up being my first song. We called it "Travelin'."

Travelin'

For 25 long years now I've been working nine to five
Trying to make a life for you but I just can't survive.
So I'll go travelin'.
Movin' on down the road.
I'm going travelin'
And I ain't gonna haul no heavy load.

You pleaded with me not to go but that just ain't no good.
Woman, I just can't stand still, got rabbit in my blood.
So I'll go travelin'.
Movin' on down the road.

I'm going travelin'
And I ain't gonna haul no heavy load.

They don't talk about the life you lead or cuss about your hair.
And cowboy boots and Levi's, Lord, is all you need to wear.
So I'll go travelin'.
Movin' on down the road.
Yes, I'm going travelin'
And I ain't gonna haul no heavy load.

CHORUS
Lord, as soon as I pack these bags of mine and throw them in that car
I'm headed back to Texas for them honkytonks and bars
Them Rednecks, Armadillos, and good ole Lone Star beer
Are just a few more reasons why I'm getting out of here
And going travelin'
Movin' on down the road
Yes, I'm going travelin'
And I ain't gonna haul no heavy load

John E. Swanger and David A. Wells, © 1978
Revelstoke, British Columbia, Canada

CHAPTER TWENTY-FIVE

HITTING THE ROAD

" 'Til I Can Gain Control Again"
Rodney Crowell © 1975

David helped me stay on task through Friday and Saturday. That evening we went back to the Big Eddy. We grabbed a table near the stage and waited for Eddie Dolan to finish his last set. He came to the table and said he told the owner that we were there to help him load out.

The owner stopped by and offered us a drink. He said, "Too late for a beer, but I'll get you a pop if you want." David declined but I took one.

As we started breaking down the stage, Eddie was throwing things into his equipment case. He called me over to the end of the stage. "You're going to need these cables. Do you have a microphone?"

"I have two Shure PE588s and mic cables," I said.

"That will do for now, but do yourself a favor and pick up a SM58 as soon as you can." He unplugged his drum machine, a Roland TR55, and handed it to me. "You'll need this also. I just bought me a new Compu-Rhythm CR800 today."

"How much for the Roland?" I asked.

"Consider it a gift. It will help get them up dancing. And that will keep you coming back for another round." He unplugged the Shure Vocal-Master along with the two tall cabinets and helped David and me to the van with them.

"I suppose you ought to know how much you'll be getting at each gig," he said.

I answered, "That would be nice."

"Vicki said she can get you $500 a week to start, but every return gig should be $600 or better."

Just before leaving, Eddie sat down and wrote out his schedule for the next couple of months so I could get in touch with him if needed.

We went back to the house. David and I loaded up our suitcases and got a cooler to haul bottles of pop and snacks. Early Sunday morning, we hit the road for the 400-kilometer trip to Calgary.

Vicki was a nice lady. I thought she would have me audition or something. But no. "I heard you on the telephone," she said, "and besides that, if Eddie says you're good, you're good."

I signed the agent's contract, and she said my first gig would be in Valemount, British Columbia, which was 530 kilometers northwest of Calgary. "Don't know if Eddie told you," she said, "but this gig pays $500 each week plus a free room. You'll have to buy your own food. It's a two-week gig. You play four hours each night, Monday through Saturday. Off Sundays. Typically you'll do four 40-minute sets each night with three 20-minute breaks between."

"Sounds great," I said.

"They will usually pay in full at the end of the contract. But sometimes they will pay at the end of each week. Do you have enough cash to cover your food for both weeks if need be?"

I answered, "I think we will be okay."

"Also, they will only supply one room, so are you okay with that?" She asked

"Yes as long as it has two beds. We are close but not that close," I said.

I asked if we would receive a contract for the hotel in Valemount, and she told me it would be mailed to the hotel manager tomorrow for him to sign. "He will make a copy for you."

With that, we hit the road again. The seven-hour drive put us in Valemount right at 8:00 p.m. The hotel owner introduced himself to me. He said, "My name is Gagnon, Phil Gagnon. But please call me Phil. And you are . . . ?"

I introduced myself and my cousin, David. I asked for a room with two beds.

Phil said, "No worries."

We unloaded and began setting up the stage. Immediately after, we went to the room. I was exhausted.

The next morning we were allowed into the bar three hours before it opened at noon. David set up the drum machine and began working out the rhythms and beats for all the songs. We made a sheet with the setting listed beside each song so I could easily program it between numbers.

Phil said he would buy me two free drinks a night, then I could buy anything else I wanted on a tab. We would settle up at the end. However, I was of the mindset, *If they are going to pay me really good money to do something I would probably do for free anyway, then I want to do the best job possible. I am going to be sober.* I thought about how Hank Williams could have been the biggest star, but he ruined his life by drinking. I wanted more than that.

The two weeks went by without any problems except, at the end of the first week, Phil called me to the office and handed me $450 cash.

I asked, "Did you take out the $50 for Vicki?"

He said ,"No, that's your responsibility."

"Vicki said I would be paid $500 a week, not $450."

He pulled out the contract and showed me. It clearly said $450. Ticked me off, but I still thought $450 was quite a bit. I thanked him.

I called Eddie right away and told him I was shorted $50 on the contract.

He said, "Don't call her. Just mail her the $100 commission next week but don't book any more gigs with her. I am sick of her doing that. She's also done it to me a few times. I am going to book myself from now on. Let me talk to a few hotels where I've played before, and, as I book them, I will tell them you will be calling. They will use you on my recommendation."

"How much will I owe you for booking me?" I asked.

"Nothing," he said.

By the end of the week, Eddie had me booked up for the next six weeks. The first gig from him was just a few miles from Revelstoke, in a town called Salmon Arm.

At the end of the second week, Phil gave me the $450 and then handed me another $100. "I'm sorry she shorted you," he said. "You were well worth the extra hundred." I told him I wasn't going to book through her anymore.

He asked, "Does that mean you won't come back here? Or can we just book it between you and me?"

I told him, "Eddie is helping me get bookings now."

He said, "I wanted Eddie back here also."

We booked me for about three months out; I called Eddie and Phil booked him for the week before me.

David and I loaded up and headed back to Revelstoke. David said he enjoyed it, but he was ready to get back to Dallas. I dropped him in Kamloops, bought him a ticket to Dallas, and then drove home. I picked up Maggie and we got back on the road.

Salmon Arm was great. Pretty much the same setup as Valemount, except I was definitely booked at $500 a week. Dick came by a couple of times during the week to hear me play. I felt bad that there was nothing for Maggie to do. She spent most of the days in the motel room, and the evenings she spent in the bar, drinking.

CHAPTER TWENTY-SIX

SUNDAY MORNING COMING DOWN

As far as the stage went, the next few months were great. Maggie, however, was getting harder and harder to deal with. With nothing to do but drink, drink she did.

I ended up renting an apartment for her in Kamloops, which we picked because it was central in B.C., and I could stop by there while traveling between gigs. However, every time I came through town she would ask to go back on the road with me. We both knew that was a disaster waiting to happen, and I wasn't likely to say yes.

One week I was coming through to go to Merritt, which was just 50 miles south of Kamloops. I was booked to play two three-day weekends there at the Val Nicola, a neighborhood pub. I spent Monday, Tuesday, and Wednesday with Maggie. Again she asked about going with me.

I told her, "The only way I would agree for you to go with me was if you were part of the show. I don't want you sitting around with nothing to do but drink."

She said, "I want to play."

Play what?" I asked.

"I don't know. I've never played anything," she answered.

"Do you think you could learn to play the bass?"

"Get me one and let's see."

We went to a pawnshop and found a Fender Jazz bass. Full scale with a natural finish and a small bass amp. We bought it and a cord. We also got a book, *How to Play Bass*.

I dropped Maggie off and headed to the gig. At closing Saturday night, I went back to Kamloops. Sunday morning, she woke me up playing her bass. Suprisingly, she sounded pretty good. We spent the next four days practicing together. Then we loaded her equipment up and headed back to Merritt. As we set up her gear, I also put a microphone on a stand in front of her. We didn't plug it in, but I told her to sing along as if it was turned on.

That day the band Sweetwater Texas was born. The gig was great. Maggie rocked. We started booking ourselves as a duo and charging $1100 a week. We rarely had a week off, and we were finding ways to promote who we were. We started printing our logo on t-shirts in our hotel rooms during the day, and then selling them from stage at night. We had a big bag full of Sweetwater Texas buttons made and sold them along with bumper stickers and posters. We printed business cards and began gathering things for the stage. We had a Texas longhorn skull we kept on stage and a huge Texas flag that we hung on the wall behind us.

We added more songs to our set list every week, and we made an elaborate stage light setup. We had our van, a 1972 Dodge customized by the owner of the bar we played in Bralorne, who also owned and operated a body shop. He had sealed the van's back doors and made it a continuous solid body as if the doors were never there. Everything we did was in some way a promotion of the band. We made our logo into a decal and posted it on the back of the van.

The next year we ended up buying another van, a 1977 Dodge conversion van. We also bought a small trailer and painted a Texas flag covering the top.

Maggie's older brother Reggie offered to hang onto our cash, because we were concerned with running around the country with so much on hand. We would drop by every couple of weeks to "make a deposit."

One night a union rep came up on stage and told me I had to join the union and pay $30 a week from my contracts, or I wouldn't be allowed to work in B.C. I told him to get off my stage or I would knock him off. The next day I got a call from Canada Immigration.

"We understand you are in the country illegally," the man said.

I told him, "I am traveling the country playing music with my Canadian wife."

He said, "I also understand you are an ex-con."

I said, "I finished up my sentence and have not been in trouble since."

"Canadian law makes no provision for ex-felons from any country," he replied.

"What do I need to do?" I asked.

"What is your schedule for the next month?"

I told him our schedule, and he said he would be coming to see us in two weeks. However, he showed up in the bar just two days later. He called us to his table, and we didn't know it was him. We thought he was just a fan. He offered to buy us a drink. We accepted. I got a Coke and Maggie got a ginger ale. Then he introduced himself as the Minister of Immigration from Toronto, Ontario.

I said, "We weren't expecting you for another week or so."

"I know," he said. "I wanted to observe you two without you knowing I was here."

"Why?" I asked.

He said "I needed to see that you were indeed married and not just playing the part so you could stay in the country."

He then pulled out his briefcase and took out a pad of papers. He pulled off the top sheet and began writing on it. He said, "I am giving you a Minister's Permit to remain in the country for six months. If you are stopped by the police or immigration, just show them this. You'll be okay."

I asked, "After six months, will I have to leave Canada?"

He answered, "No. I am also giving you my card. Call me in five months and let me know where you will be, and I will send you another permit." We thanked him and he left.

Six months later he did as he said he would. Then six months after that, he instead sent me a five-year permit.

....

CHAPTER TWENTY-SEVEN

PAPA WAS A ROLLING STONE?

Maggie and I were drifting further apart. I was also feeling I had no family in Texas that cared for me. I began to really want to know who my birth father was.

My mother had always described my father as "a no-good, worthless, abusive, drunken, lazy drifter who couldn't hold a job." My older sister, Evelyn, said he would beat us with a light cord. She said he beat me the most.

Perhaps my only memories of him were tainted by the hatred my mother and older sister had for him. Or perhaps my memories of abuse were real. I couldn't tell. Either way I was at a place in my life where I felt I had to find him. I didn't want anything, I just wanted to look him in the eye. I wanted to know that I did, indeed, have a father.

I set out on a search to find him. I really didn't have much to go on, just his name and that he was born in Shulls Mills, North Carolina. I also knew he lived in Detroit before he met my mom in 1948.

I started by calling information for Detroit. "No such number." Then with a map I began calling all the small towns around Detroit. "No such number," was the response, over and over again. Finally I called information in Roseville, Michigan. "I'm sorry, that's a non-published number." So I knew what town he was in: Roseville.

I knew my sister Evelyn wasn't interested in meeting him. My older brother, Donnie, had always said, "If I ever find him, I'm going to kick his ass." So I called my younger brother, David, in Tulsa, Oklahoma.

"David, I'm going to Detroit to find Jack. Do you want to come with me?"

"Yes," he said.

I bought airline tickets to Detroit for David and me and told David I would meet him at his gate. We flew in to Detroit Metropolitan Airport on Wednesday, July 16, 1980. I thought, *I had no idea Detroit was such a busy place*. The airport was packed. It took me forever to get to the gate where David was coming in.

Then I heard a voice on the loudspeaker announce, "Welcome to Detroit's Metropolitan Airport. We especially want to welcome all the delegates and presidential candidates to the 1980 Republican National Convention."

David arrived and I was surprised that he had Marsha, his wife, with him. We grabbed their bags and headed off to pick up the rental car I had (thankfully) reserved.

We drove to Roseville and started looking for a motel. It made me wish I had booked it in advance also. Politicians had absorbed virtually every room within miles of the convention. Finally we found a really small and run-down room. One room, with one bed. I slept on the floor. It was extremely hot, and we had no air conditioner. We slept with the door open to try to get a bit of draft flowing through.

The next morning we went to eat some breakfast. Then we drove to the electric utility company and walked up to the counter. The lady said, "May I help you?"

"Yes I'm here to pay my father's power bill."

She asked, "What's the address?"

I said, "I really forgot to ask. We are visiting from out of town."

I pointed out the door and waved my hand left then right and said "He lives about three blocks up that way and then four blocks to the right."

She looked at the $40 I had in my hand.

Then she said, "What is your father's name?"

I leaned over the counter so I could get a better look as she typed into the computer. "Jack Swanger, ma'am."

As she typed, "17283 Ivanhoe St., Roseville, Michigan, 48066" popped up on the screen.

She said, "That will be $65."

I stuffed the cash back in my pocket and said, "We'll have to come back with more money. Sorry."

As we walked out the door, I wrote the address down and handed it to David. We got in the car, pulled out the map, and headed to the address. Once there, we parked down the street from the house and sat and watched for quite a while. About an hour later we saw a pickup truck pull into the driveway. An older man, who we assumed was Jack, got out and went inside.

I turned to David and said, "Are you ready for this?"

He said, "Yes."

Marsha waited in the car, while David and I walked to the door. I started getting nervous. We knocked on the door and he answered. He looked out through the screen door at David and said, "You are David."

Then he looked at me and said, "And you must be Duck. You were always my favorite." I was shocked that, after twenty-three years, he recognized us. Not only as his kids, but which ones. I was also both pleased and saddened because he said, "You were my favorite." Pleased, but I felt bad for David. It was a bit awkward.

Just then his wife came out and asked, "Who the hell are these two?"

"They are my sons," Jack told her.

She instantly became angry and screamed, "Get the hell out of here."

I told Jack we didn't want anything other than to just see him. "We are leaving. Don't want to cause problems." We started walking back to the car.

"Well, we saw him," I told David. "But that's all. You want to go see New York? We are pretty close and we both have almost two weeks."

David said, "Might as well." Just as we reached the car, Jack's wife screeched out of the driveway in the truck.

She yelled, "You can go back to the house and visit with him. But I will be back in an hour. Be gone by then."

The three of us walked back to the house. Jack invited us in. He sat four cups on the kitchen table and poured us some coffee. The next hour went by with us asking questions and him answering as best he could. I have always had a b.s. meter within me and can usually tell when someone is lying. I felt Jack was trying as best he could to be honest. When I asked why he left my mom, he was frank. "It wasn't her fault, and it wasn't my fault. It just started falling apart."

Then he looked at David and said, "Actually, David, when you were born, I mistakenly thought you weren't mine. I thought your mom was cheating on me. I look at you now, though, and I clearly see how wrong I was."

Again my heart was breaking for David. Sometimes brutal honesty can be more than brutal. It looked like David was beginning to tear up.

Jack told us his wife, Myrtle, didn't know he was married before or that he had kids. She was on her way back. It was time to leave. Then he said, "Come with me."

We walked to his car, and he drove us to where he worked. We got out at ACCO, American Chain and Cable, where he was a welder. "I want to show you boys something," he said. He opened up his locker, and on the back wall were photos of all four of us kids: Donnie, Evelyn, me, and David.

"I just wanted you to know that I never forgot you, and I think of you every day."

Then he showed us an eagle he had tattooed on his forearm. You could faintly see our four names behind the cover-up tattoo. He said he always wanted to tell Myrtle but was waiting for the right time.

"I guess it never was the right time," I added.

We drove back to his house, said goodbye, and were heading across the lawn when Myrtle came out. "You three might as well stay for supper," she said. "But that's it. Then you are out of here."

I couldn't help but think she was softening up. Things were certainly getting less stressful. As dinner ended she asked where we were staying. We told her about the motel.

She said, "There is no sense paying for that place. Just grab your things. You might as well hang out here." We ended up staying there for the entire time we were in Detroit.

CHAPTER TWENTY-EIGHT

AGAINST THE WIND

I felt like the band was getting stronger every week we played. But I also felt that Maggie and I were continuing to drift further apart. There was certainly no shortage of groupies. Maggie had hers and I had mine. I began to feel like Maggie was more like a sister than a wife. It was as if I loved her, but I wasn't in love with her. I would fight to protect her, but we were more like business partners than husband and wife. Obviously the free-love sexual revolution thing wasn't working for us.

After a little more than four years on the road, one night I was standing on stage playing a song. I glanced over at the bass player and my brain went tilt. It was like: *That's your* wife.

We finished the song, and I said, "Maggie, we need to talk after this set."

We sat down and I looked at her. "We need to get a divorce," I said.

She responded, "What?"

"A divorce," I said.

"Why?"

"What if you find someone you fall in love with? Or what if I do?"

"I suppose you're right," she said.

Later that night, after we were in our hotel room, we talked. We decided we would play out the remainder of the schedule but not book anything else. We had about four more months of bookings ahead.

We made it through the schedule, and before the last gig we stopped by Revelstoke to pick up the other van. Then we dropped by Reggie's house to get our cash and headed to Lumby for the last gig.

It was strange driving there without Maggie, who was in the other van. We stopped for lunch and went over the lyrics of some new songs we were adding to the portfolio:

"Fire on the Mountain," Marshall Tucker Band

"Tequila Sunrise," The Eagles

"Against the Wind," Bob Seger

We pulled into Lumby for the last gig of Sweetwater Texas. They were having the World Hang Gliding Championship competition there that week. We met several of the contestants from around the world in the bar. Several asked us to join in the celebrations during the day, and they offered to take us up on tandem flights. Lumby is one of the world's most fitting places for hang gliding. It has a high peak with a sudden drop-off right into the thermals where you can soar for a half hour or more.

We spent the week playing in the bar at night and watching the competition during the day. The competition ended on Friday, and some of the contestants stayed to enjoy the mountain. Saturday morning I went up with one of the instructors.

He strapped me in and said, "Close your eyes and run with me. Don't stop running." We ran off the side of the mountain and caught a thermal right away. As soon as we cleared land, he swung me from behind him to right by his side.

I asked him, "Why did you ask me to close my eyes?"

"Because a lot of people get scared and stop running," he said. "Then we fall off the mountain."

I have to say I have never experienced anything as peaceful as hang gliding. Defying gravity as if it didn't even exist. As soon as we landed I asked about going up again. "That was a free one," he said, "but if you want to go back up, it'll cost you $40—but really, I have to go, so if you want any more flying you'll have to hit up one of the others. They all charge $40."

For four and a half years we had started and ended every night with "Good Hearted Woman," but I decided to end our last night with my own song: "When the Sun Comes Up in Dallas."

I think we were both teary-eyed by the end of the song. We knew it was over and it needed to be. But it still hurt. We sat down before breaking down the stage and loading the equipment.

"You okay, Maggie?" I asked.

"I will be," she said.

We decided she would take the older van and go back to Revelstoke. She would keep all the household things, and I would keep the stage gear. We also agreed that we would get together in a few months and see if there was anything left of our marriage worth salvaging.

I told her I was going to Tulsa where my younger brother David lived. She reached through the window of the van, picked up something off the seat, and handed me my prison photo. "You better hang onto this," she said, "since I won't be there to keep you in line."

As I drove away, I started thinking back on the nearly seven years we were together. *Maggie was the first girl to care about me as a person. I might have just been so desperate to find someone, anyone, to care that I simply latched onto her and hung on . . .*

When the Sun Comes Up in Dallas
CHORUS
When the sun comes up in Dallas,
It'll be settin' down on me.
And when it up and shows itself again,
Just no tellin' where I'll be.

VERSE 1
Well, I tried to rearrange my thoughts
And get her off my mind.
But I keep thinkin' bout all the things I took
And the things I left behind.

BRIDGE
I walked along the river banks

And down the railroad track.
At times I reminisced a bit
But never thought of going back.

VERSE 2
But she took her place in my mind that
I didn't know was there.
So now I'm lying to myself
By saying I don't care.

REPEAT VERSE 1
Well, I tried to rearrange my thoughts
And get her off my mind.
But I keep thinkin' bout all the things I took
And the things I left behind.

VERSE 3
When everything was going right
I up and walked away.
I don't know why I left that girl
But I knew I couldn't stay.

VERSE 4
Leavin' is the kind of thing
No one can understand.
But like Waylon 'til the day I die,
I guess I'll be a ramblin' man.

REPEAT CHORUS X2
When the sun comes up in Dallas,
It'll be settin' down on me.
And when it up and shows itself again,
Just no tellin' where I'll be.

John Swanger, © 1981

CHAPTER TWENTY-NINE

A NEW CHAPTER

The end of my marriage obviously brought the end of Sweetwater Texas, which also meant I was to leave Canada. I headed to Oklahoma, only because my younger brother David lived there.

The long drive was just what I needed to settle things within myself and to begin the process of closing a chapter of my life. I pulled onto the highway and headed south. As I drove, I speculated about what my future would hold. I was a survivor, so whatever came my way I was confident I could handle it. I hurried to the border but then took my time making it to Tulsa. Four days later, I crossed the state line into Oklahoma.

It was late on a Tuesday evening when I pulled into Tulsa. I was tired, but I wanted to see David, so I headed over to his house. Marsha and the kids were in bed. David made coffee and we sat down to talk.

He asked, "What happened? You and Maggie always got along so great."

I answered, "We never fought. We just grew apart. She was my best friend and my bass player, but there wasn't any romance left. I still love her, but I'm not *in* love with her. Mainly, we got burned out from being on the road too long. We were together 24/7. Living together, playing together, and working together. She became more like a sister than a wife."

David's question, "You going to get divorced?" brought my response, "We decided to give it a three-month break and then get back together to see if there is anything left. Then we'll decide."

David brought out a pillow and some blankets, and I made a bed of the couch. I woke up to the smell of bacon. Marsha stuck her head out of the kitchen door.

"I'm making your favorite," she called. "Biscuits and gravy. With eggs and bacon."

I was pleased. I wouldn't say that biscuit and gravy were my favorite, but Marsha's biscuits and gravy were the best I had ever eaten. She made her biscuits from scratch and had a way with the gravy that was incomparable. Simply the best.

For the first time in years, I felt like I was sitting in a house full of people who loved me—even the kids, Stephanie and James David. I felt like I was home.

Over breakfast, I filled Marsha in. She asked what my plans were. "To not ever go on the road again," I answered.

David said, "You can stay here as long as you want."

I told him I would start looking for a place right away. I loved them, but the last thing I wanted was to be a burden on anyone. David also told me that his work, Western Uniform, was always looking for people. I followed him to the warehouse and filled out the application. They interviewed me right away and hired me.

I told them, "In three months, I will need to take a week off." That would be the week Maggie would be coming to town.

Max, the supervisor, said, "No problem."

I spent the next week riding with David as he trained me. I helped him with his route and he taught me everything I needed to know to be a ragman. We delivered shop towels and floor mats and uniforms to all the automotive, industrial, and machine shops in and around Tulsa.

Marsha was serving cocktails at The Cellar, a bar in a strip mall. There were actually nine topless bars and two nude clubs, all in the same strip mall, at 21st and Mingo in southeast Tulsa. Marsha introduced me to Cricket, a former dancer who also used to wait tables there.

Cricket told me she had a son who was learning the guitar and was looking to join a band. I was so disillusioned by the previous four and a half years on the road that I sold her all my stage equipment for $3,000, just to make certain I would never entertain the idea of hitting the road again. I sold her everything, including the PA system, the stage gear, the lighting equipment, the mics, and my two electric guitars, a 1966 Telecaster and a 1968 Stratocaster. All in all, I think it was about $12,000 worth of gear. Everything except my acoustic guitar and Maggie's bass.

Within three weeks, I was kicking myself in the butt as the urge to return to the road began to eat at me.

Cricket became a friend. She wasn't someone I was attracted to, but she was my friend. She introduced me to the president and vice president of the Tulsa chapter of the Mongols motorcycle club. Chief was the president and his younger brother Budd was the VP. They owned Tulsa Harley Davidson and were frequent customers at the strip. I hung out there frequently with them.

I had bought a 1977 Honda 750cc and immediately took it home and tore it apart in the dining room to begin rebuilding it. I took the tank and side covers to a body shop, and they painted them brown for me. I had the fenders and all the brackets re-chromed. I also took the seat to an upholstery shop, and they recovered it. I traded shop rags and floor mats for all the work. Finally, I got it back together.

Budd and Chief said they would love to have me ride with them, but they said I would have to get a real motorcycle first, meaning a Harley.

I can't tell you why, but I started drinking—and began snorting cocaine.

I traded my conversion van at a car lot for a 1973 MGB convertible. Right away my MGB broke down, and I had to find a mechanic. The guy I bought cocaine from sent me to his friend. He ended up becoming not just my mechanic but my new dealer as well. He sold much larger quantities. I would often buy an eight-ball—about 3.5 grams—from him. Most cocaine in Tulsa was Clorox testing at about twenty-five to thirty percent. The first eight-ball I bought from Mark tested out at sixty-five percent.

I ended up taking half for myself and cutting the other half with vitamin B12 and selling it to the dancers at the strip, and to Budd and Chief. They were impressed, because even after cutting it, it still tested out higher than anything else in town. They began asking for more. Budd introduced me to a couple of dealers who were both Mongols. I started buying ounces from Mark and selling them half, once I stepped on it. The money started rolling in.

I met a couple of other bikers at the strip from Los Paisanos, another outlaw motorcycle club from California. They were in town to work on setting up a Tulsa chapter. They also were looking to buy coke. I sold them one of my cut ounces for $2,200. Since I was paying two thousand dollars an ounce and cutting it in half, I was making a great profit.

❖ ❖ ❖

When Maggie came to town, we decided to go ahead with the divorce. I gave her the bass I had taken when I left Canada. I wondered why I hadn't given it to her before I left. I quit working at Western Uniform the day she got to town.

The owners of the strip, Tiger and her husband Pete, hired me as a bouncer. I actually walked in after dropping Maggie at the airport. Tiger came to my table and said "We fired a couple of bouncers today. Do you need a job?"

"Yes, I do," I answered. "How much does it pay?"

She said, "I'll pay you $70 a shift. How many can you work a week?"

"I suppose I can work five or six." She asked me to start the next evening.

Within two weeks I was asked to manage the bouncers. Tiger bumped my pay to $85 a shift. I would get there and meet with all the bouncers and assign them to each bar for the evening. We needed to make sure each club had two bouncers, except for The Cellar and Suds & Jugs. They needed three because at times the crowds there were rowdier than the others.

I told David I was working at the strip and he said to be careful. "Just a few months ago there was a big shootout at Suds & Jugs. Two rival biker clubs got in a fight and three people got shot. Two died." I promised him I would be careful.

Marsha quit working there. Cricket came back to work, and soon Tiger asked me to start assigning the dancers also.

On just the second night there, Tiger called me to the parking lot. There were three Christian men out there handing out tracts and inviting men to their church. I asked them to leave but they refused.

I said to them, "I don't stand on the steps of your business trying to steal your customers. Don't you come here and try to steal mine."

One of them said, "Jesus loves you."

I answered, "How would you like it if I came to your church and started shouting 'Free beer at the titty bar, so get out of here'?" They looked at me like they were offended that I said *titty*. I said, "Leave now."

They didn't. I slapped one of them and jumped at the other two as they ran for their cars. Tiger and I headed back into the bar.

CHAPTER THIRTY

....

WHO IS THIS GUY?

Having a protective instinct for women, I was always quick to jump in and defend the girls. I wouldn't hesitate to bust a guy up and throw him out if he was disrespectful in any way to one of them. Soon the dancers all wanted to dance in whichever club I was working in, for no reason other than that they knew I would protect them.

The main rule I enforced with the bouncers was this:

If you lose a fight, you're fired.
Nothing personal. But I hired you to be in control of the bar.
If someone whips your butt, who's in control?

I got to the point where I wasn't afraid of anyone. As each person walked into the bar, I would size them up, just like casing out a bank before robbing it. I would ask myself, *What will it take to whip the guy?* For some, it was a simple roundhouse to the nose. For others, a punch to the mouth. And still others, it was, *I can just bitch slap that one.*

There were times when someone would pull a knife on me. I wouldn't hesitate at all. I would knock them down and put their knife in my pocket. When I got home I would stab the knife into my front door. It was like my trophy case. Eventually I had seventeen knives stuck in there, and a baseball bat sitting by the door that some punk pulled on me.

One of the girls I was dating was named Carla. She was Budd's old lady. Dangerous move on my part, but still, I dabbled there. There were even times when I went to their house when Budd was out of town. Once we went to Cricket's house and she went off on us. She knew Carla was

Budd's girl and said she didn't want me bringing heat around her place. We left.

Once I asked Carla, "I know how Budd is around me. I think he likes me, but what does Budd say to you about me?"

She said, "He calls you 'that Italian-looking dude.'"

I don't know where that came from.

I asked, "Do you really think he is just keeping me around because I get them the coke they need?"

She answered, "He said he likes you and wished you could ride with them."

Often, as Chief and Budd brought others to the bars, they would park their bikes right by the front door. While they were inside, I would pour a spot of oil under a couple of them. Everyone knew that Harleys were notorious for leaking.

They would come out and start cussing. "Damn it, I just overhauled that thing." I couldn't help it, I would start laughing and give it away.

I also at times told them, "Don't park too close to my motorcycle. I don't want you to splatter oil on it."

Their response was always, "You would have to actually own a real motorcycle first."

One of my bouncers was named Eddie. He wore a t-shirt that said ASSHOLE on the front, so he became known as Asshole Eddie. He had worked there longer than me, and at times he complained that he should have gotten the manager's job instead of me.

Once I was walking from bar to bar and I saw Pete, Tiger's husband, coming out of one of the bars. I was standing in the doorway of the bar next to it as three guys stepped out of the bar where Peter was and headed over to mine. Pete was looked at me and shook his head in a way that told me, *Don't let them in.*

As they tried to walk past me into the bar, I put my hand up. "Time to go home, guys. You are done here for the night."

One of the three tried to push past me. I knocked him out. Then the second stepped up. I knocked him out also. The third started to move. "Step right up," I said. "I have a good pile growing."

I just grabbed him by the throat and asked which car was his. I threw him in it and dragged both the others to the car and threw them in the back seat.

Then I walked on down to the first bar on the strip, Suds & Jugs, where the bartender handed me a beer. I saw Budd sitting at a table alone. I nodded and said "Hi."

Just then the door flew open and Asshole Eddie walked in. He was pissed. I could see he was heading my way. I was concerned because I knew Budd had been friends with Eddie long before I was around.

Eddie said, "I want to know who all just beat up my friends."

I said, "First of all, Pete told me not to let them in, so I stopped them from coming in. Second, 'who all?' was just me. And third, who the hell are you to tell me you don't like the way I do my job? Remember, you work for me, Eddie. Not the other way around."

Then Eddie said, "Get up, you need to go back down there and finish this."

I thought, *Crap, now I've got to fight these three guys* and *Asshole*.

Just then Budd stood up and said, "Hey, Asshole. There ain't gonna be no Rat Packin'. If there is, I'm with the Italian-looking dude." That brought a smile to my face.

We walked down to where their car was parked and again I told them to leave. All three got out and started walking my way.

The biggest of the three said, "I want to know who is going to pay to replace my tooth you knocked out."

Before I could speak, Budd said, "If someone knocks my tooth out, I sure ain't going to push him to knock more out."

I added, "Right now you have time to back out and leave. But I'm telling you. If you step up on that curb, I'm going to tear you all a new one. So think about it."

They stopped, got back in their car, and left.

I turned to Eddie and said, "You're fired. Leave the strip now."

He left, and Budd and I walked back to Suds & Jugs.

One night Budd and Chief came into the strip and said they'd decided they wanted me to start riding with them. "You can hang with us," Budd said, "but you can't prospect until you get a Harley. John, you are just a couple of steps away from becoming a Mongol. A family member."

Chief said, "What you are is what we call a 'hang around.' It's what everyone is just before prospecting."

I said, "So I go on runs with you guys?"

They both said, "Yes, exactly."

I had moved into a small, older apartment. My manager was one of my biker friends, Danny Woodley. There was a QuickTrip, a convenience store, right behind the apartments. I began to stop in there every night on my way home, either for cigarettes or for a six-pack. To be honest, it was more a thrill to see the look on the clerk's face when I would stop in every night, and he could see I had another girl on the back of my motorcycle.

I would walk in and say, "What's happening, Jack?"

He would always respond, "You are, John."

I figured, *He must think I am pretty cool. He's always saying that I am what's happening.* I stopped by there almost every night for a couple of months. He was really the only person I knew who wasn't in the life. He wasn't a biker, a dealer, an addict, a stripper, or a drunk customer. He was a bit of a nerd, but he was also a bit of a break from my life. Sometimes we would talk a few minutes before I called it a night.

My drinking began to get out of control. I was getting drunk almost every night. And doing coke meant I could drink even more. One evening, when I was drunk, I tripped over the coffee table and crashed into the end table, where I had my prison photo sitting. I broke it, and the pieces of the frame fell to the floor. The next morning, I cleaned it up and put the photo away. I thought I would reframe it and put it back by the door where it belonged.

I went to a couple of AA meetings, but they did nothing for me. The more I tried to quit, the more I drank. My cocaine use also kept escalating. Soon I was buying almost as much coke for myself as I was for my dealers.

Hanging out with the Mongols didn't help with my need to tone down my drinking. I went on a couple of runs to Kansas to help them with some parts they were buying. I also helped set up a big party for some prospects who were getting patched in.

I played pool a lot, usually for no more than a couple of dollars per game. I had a friend named Larry who looked kind of like a thin Benjamin Franklin. He was about forty with long hair, but bald on top, and wore really old-fashioned glasses. With the exception of Willie Mosconi, he was without a doubt the best pool player I had ever known. He played nine ball. He would give me the eight, which meant if I made the eight or nine I won, while he had to make the nine to win. Others, he would give them the six or seven.

Larry would walk into the bar and look at me to point out who was a high roller. I would, and he would start playing them. I kept track in my head of how much he would win off them, even to the number of quarters he dropped in the table. When he was finished, he would stop by on his way out and give me half. He never shorted me, not even a quarter.

One evening I was in The Cellar playing pool against another bouncer. We were finishing up a game of nine ball when a woman I had never met before walked in and came straight over to the pool table.

She said, "I'll play any guy in here for twenty bucks a game."

I thought, *I don't know who she is but it would be worth it just to see if she could beat me.*

She started racking the balls for nine ball, and I chalked up my stick. I broke and the nine shot over into the side pocket as she was opening her pool case. I smiled because I had never made the nine on the break before. She threw a twenty to my end of the table and re-racked.

She said, "Using the ten for the nine this time, okay?"

I said, "Of course."

I re-chalked as she racked. By now she was screwing her stick together. I broke. Once again the nine shot into the side pocket. She tossed me another twenty, saying, "You're too f&@#n' lucky." She put her cue back in its case and walked out. Just then a couple other pool players came to the table.

One of them, a bouncer named Derik, said, "Do you know who that was?"

I said, "I have no idea."

Derik said, "That, my friend, was Robin Bell. A world contender in women's nine ball.

"How do you know?" I asked.

He said, "I just saw her on TV last week, and I checked her ID as she came in."

"Thanks for not telling me." I said. "If I had known, I would probably be in the hole and still trying to beat her."

Suds & Jugs had become the slowest bar on the strip. I convinced Tiger to let me close it down, repaint it, and then reopen it as a male strip joint. I called it The Kickstand. I auditioned about one hundred dancers just to find twenty who were straight. I decided I didn't want gay guys dancing for women. It seemed kind of like false advertising.

I also hired Danny Woodley. He was big and good-looking but he was clumsy. I taught him how to dance, and I taught him how to strip. We opened The Kickstand and were packed the first night. I was surprised to see that most of our customers were the strippers from the other bars.

I felt I could handle everyone who came into all the bars, with the exception of Tony, a large black man, who was about 6'3" and 250 pounds. He was built like a V. I kept telling myself, *That's the guy who's going to take my job.* I still wasn't afraid of him; I just didn't think I could take him. So I did the best thing I could think of. I became his friend.

I started dropping by at noon to assign the bouncers and dancers. Then I would come back in at 4:00 P.M. for the evening shift every day except Tuesday, which I took off.

CHAPTER THIRTY-ONE

FIGHTING FOR MY LIFE

Monday, January 31, 1983

One evening I was walking from bar to bar and stopped into The Cellar. There in the middle of the floor was Tony, with Tiger holding her hands up on his chest. Four bouncers were gathered around them in a circle.

Tony was yelling over Tiger at one of the girls standing behind her. "You're gonna' work for me, or I'm gonna' kill you."

Tiger was saying, "Calm down, Tony."

Tony was what we called a tennis shoe pimp. There were the Huggy Bear types who sweet-talked girls into working for them. The tennis shoe pimps wouldn't bother with the romance, they were strictly bulldogs, operating on threats instead of finesse. They wouldn't even dress up; that's why they were called tennis shoe pimps.

It was strange seeing Tiger with both hands up on Tony's chest. He was massive, and she was so little. I was walking across the floor towards them when all of a sudden Tony reached into his pocket and pulled out a gun. He reached over with his left hand and cocked it. As he pulled it up and pointed it at the girl behind Tiger, I jumped on his back and started hitting him in the face.

We cut a path across the bar like a tornado, tables falling over, people screaming and running, pitchers of beer flipping through the air as we were slugging it out. I watched all four bouncers hit the back door.

Somehow I had gotten hit over the head with the gun, and I began to get a little cloudy. I just kept pounding on him.

Tony was down and I was sitting on his chest, thinking, *I need to knock him out, because if I pass out he is going to kill me.*

Somehow I got his gun and shoved it in my back pocket. Just then I saw a big ol' banana knife reach in and lay across Tony's neck. The hand that held it belonged to a short, thin biker I had never met. He had long black braids down his back, a Fu Man Chu moustache, and a red bandana tied around his forehead. He definitely looked Mexican.

He looked at me and said with a thick Mexican accent, "You look like you could use a break, man."

I said, "Yeah, I could."

He said to me, "Go ahead, I got him."

Then he looked at Tony, and said "You move and I'm gonna put your neck in your pocket."

I walked over to the bar and Tiger drew me a beer. I downed it, then did a couple of lines of coke off the end of the bar. I shook my head a few times to get the cobwebs out, then headed back to Tony. I sat back on his chest.

Mr. Banana Knife said, "You ready?"

I nodded, then he pulled the knife back, and I started pounding on Tony again. I knocked him out. Then Tiger brought me some flex-cuffs from behind the bar.

I cuffed his hands and his feet, then we dragged him out back to let him cool off a bit. We would always lay them in the alley for a couple of hours, then go out and cut them loose.

I walked back in ready to fire the four bouncers, but Tiger was already on it. They were mostly glad to go. Sometimes you need to face the fact that your call in life isn't as easy as you think.

I grabbed two bottles of Coors and walked over to Mr. Banana Knife. First thing I did was offer him a job. "Ever thought of being a bouncer?" I asked.

He said, "I don't think I'm big enough."

I then asked, "What's your name?"

"James Hughes."

I replied, "No need to b.s. me, man. That's the whitest name in the book, and you are obviously Mexican."

"No, actually I'm half Hawaiian and half Native American—Navajo. My dad was James Hughes, and I am James Hughes, Jr. But," he said as he smiled, "if you call me Junior I'll put your neck in Tony's pocket."

"But why do you sound Mexican?" I asked.

"I like to keep 'em guessing," he said.

"Either way, man, thanks for the help. You might actually have saved my butt tonight,"

I announced that the bar was closed for the evening and told everyone to head out. I also told Hughes that his drinks were on me next time he came in. With that, I ushered everyone to the door. Tiger thanked me, and I got on my motorcycle and rode off. As I exited the parking lot, I could see James still kicking his bike. Heading to the apartment, I realized that I had forgotten to cut Tony loose.

I laughed, and then said out loud, "Serves him right."

I smoked my last cigarette, tossed the pack, then pulled into the QuickTrip. As soon as I did, I realized I had just blown my image. *Here I am without a girl, and the nerd is waving at me to come in.*

Jack said, "I see you're alone tonight. Let me buy you a cup of coffee."

I bought a six-pack and a couple packs of Camel Filters, then leaned on the counter sipping on a cup of nasty coffee while Jack talked.

"Do you know why I'm in Tulsa?" he asked.

I answered, "I can see, can't I? You work at a convenience store."

He said, "True. But the real reason I'm here is that I'm going to college and I work here just to pay the bills and cover my tuition."

"Where do you go to college?" I asked.

"A little college called Rhema in Broken Arrow, about twenty miles from here," he answered.

I asked, "What the heck is a Rhema?"

"It's a Christian college."

The hair stood up on my neck. I couldn't stand Christians. I saw them as weak, stupid people. Not a fan of people pushing their beliefs on others. *If this dude had told me a couple of months ago that he was a Christian,* I thought, *I would never have come back in here.*

I think Jack saw the grimace on my face. "That coffee is pretty old," he said. "Let me make a fresh pot." He grabbed my cup and tossed it, then quickly made more and poured me some.

I thought, *I just handled the toughest guy in the world. And he had a gun. I can handle this wimpy Christian dude.* "That's cool," I said, "I can deal with that."

He said, "I've been telling my wife about you and she thinks you sound pretty cool. We want to invite you over for dinner tomorrow. Tuesday is my night off and it's your night off also. How would you like a home-cooked meal?"

I just stood there thinking about how to get out of there without becoming offensive.

"John," he said, "when was the last time you had a home-cooked meal?"

"Does prison count? Cause if not, I'm not sure I ever had one."

"Come. It'll be fun. Your friend Danny Woodley will be there." I thought I'd go, just to give Danny a hard time about hanging with a Christian. Then Jack added, "By the way, James Hughes will be there also."

I thought, *I understand he knows Danny. After all, he lives right behind the store, where I live. But how the hell does he know James Hughes? And how does he know that I know James Hughes? I left the bar before James did—and I just met him tonight.* I was starting to freak out a bit. I thought about the Mongols and the Paisanos. I had helped a guy steal one of the Paisanos motorcycles and sell it to the Mongols. I knew Danny was friends with Budd and Chief. And James certainly did look Mexican. *This could be a set up.*

But never being one to back down, I said, "I'll be there. What time and where?"

Jack wrote down the address and told me 6:30 as he handed it to me.

I hopped on my bike and rode around the building to my apartment, dropped the kickstand, and went up the three short steps to my door. As I walked in, I turned around and grabbed one of the knives from the door. I pulled it out and stabbed it back in—but through the trigger hole of my newest trophy, a Smith & Wesson 9mm automatic.

I turned my recliner around so I could sit and look at the gun hanging on the door, opened a beer, and sat down. The next hours were spent telling myself how tough I was. After all, I had just defeated the biggest guy in the world. And he'd had a gun.

Once I had consumed half of the six-pack, I began to doubt myself. *Was I really that good? Or was I just lucky?* The smallest wimp could kill the biggest of the big with one of those. I began to obsess with how close I had actually come to losing my life. Was James Hughes a real human? Or was he an angel?

I thought about Tiger and that poor girl behind her. While I truly did have an instinct to protect women, I had lost my love for them. Women had just become objects to me. Perhaps it was the sexual revolution or just from working on the strip, or a combination of both. I was amazed how I saw the prettiest women in the world walk into the strip and the ugliest women in the world walk out. It only took a couple of months, and they were altered. Was it the drugs? Was it the disregard for their self-respect? They walked in glowing, with smiles on their faces. They walked out like empty shells.

I truly tried to care for several of the girls, but ended up giving up on them. I felt like a fraud. I wanted to love them and help them but I, too, used them. It pained me to see so many girls who felt like sex was all they had to offer the world.

And me. Where had I gone wrong? I had been doing so good. And now? I thought about my prison photo. Where was it? I hadn't seen it in months. I hadn't even thought about it.

I got up and looked through my boxes for it, finally finding it in a manila file folder. I took out the photo and sat back down to look at it. It no longer held the magic I needed to keep me on track.

I finished the other three bottles, then tried to sleep. I tossed and turned for a bit, then finally got back up and rode to Denny's for some breakfast.

A group of dancers and a couple of bouncers from the strip were there and invited me to join them. I sat down and ordered bacon and eggs.

There was a ruckus at the other end of the restaurant. Our waitress said, "Try to ignore it. It's just the dishwasher. He's pissed at the manager."

"Why?" I asked.

She said, "He came in late and the manager told him to go home. Now he's worried that he'll lose his job and get sent back to prison."

Just then the dishwasher started yelling, "I'll whip any mother f&$%r in this restaurant. Anyone."

I stood up, looked across the restaurant at him, and said, "Excuse me. Sir? I'd like to try."

He looked at me and stopped. Then he yelled out, "Any mother f&$%r at this end of the restaurant? Anyone." With that, we all laughed, then he walked out. Everything calmed down. I ate my breakfast then headed back to the house.

Paul Stavenjord

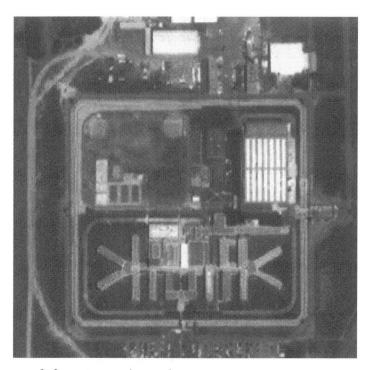

A gift from Dr. Barbara Bliss, FCI Lompoc, 1975

Peter and Lillian

Seattle Promo
Poster, 1976

JOHN SWANGER

Wanted Poster, Seattle, 1977

Sweetwater Texas Button

Jack Swanger's Dog Tags, 1980

Jack and John, 1952

Jack Swanger and Duck 1952

John, Jack, and David, 1980

CHAPTER THIRTY-TWO

TWO QUESTIONS

Tuesday, February 1, 1983

I woke up at the crack of noon and reached for a cigarette. Then I drank the corners out of the six bottles I'd consumed the night before. I fumbled around, found my wallet, and pulled a shirt on. I walked around the building to the QuikTrip and bought a coffee and an apple fritter. Sitting on the curb by the store, I thought about what had happened the night before.

Two sips later, I walked back into the store and added cream to the coffee. *I wish I hadn't told Jack I would come to his house tonight,* I thought. *But I did, so I guess I'm going.*

I jumped into my MG and drove off. I pulled into the strip on my day off and walked into Kitty's. I looked around and spotted a girl who wasn't too tough on the eyes. I called out, "Brenda!"

She turned to me and said, "Yeah?"

I said, "You want to move in with me?"

She said, "I certainly do."

She grabbed her little bag of G-strings and we headed to the door. We pulled out, and I realized that having a woman live with you meant you would need to have certain things in your house. "We need to stop at Walmart to pick up some stuff," I said.

We were in Walmart for roughly an hour and a half. We emerged with all the necessities: beer, toilet paper, dishes, towels, ice-cube trays, a toilet brush, and food. Lots of food. We even bought a couple of those rugs for the bathroom floor and a shower curtain. We found an alarm clock and a mirror for the bathroom.

Then we went to Denny's for lunch. Steak and eggs. Coffee and orange juice. She just ordered oatmeal. I asked why. She said, "I don't have any cash on me."

I said, "I'm buying. This isn't a financial partnership, its life." She said, "Okay," but then she only added cinnamon toast to her order.

We got home about four and started unloading the car. We had just gotten all the groceries put away when I remembered I had to go to Jack's. I wasn't going to tell her I was going to a Christian's house. I had already taken one severe blow to my street cred this week, and it was only Tuesday. I certainly couldn't afford another.

I said, "Make yourself at home, Brenda. I have to go meet some of my guys. The beer is in the fridge, weed is in the cabinet, and there's coke in the freezer. I'll be back later."

I jumped on my bike and headed out. Along the way, my mind started racing. I really didn't want to be hanging out with Christians. Christian men were all nerds with their short hair and their collared shirts. Christian music sucked. Christian women were all ugly. They had no makeup, dresses down to the ankles, kind of a blue haze to their hair, and one of those little pins on their dress—an old ivory carving of women, a cameo, that's what it was called. And Christian homes all sucked. There were crosses on every wall, Bibles on every table, and one of those plastic pictures of Jesus that move as you walk by. You look at it and Jesus is on the cross, then you take two steps and bam, he's kneeling in the garden. Then there's that other one of Jesus where his eyes follow you as you walk across the floor. That was just too freaky. I wanted nothing to do with any of it.

And I thought about the questions. I always had two questions to ask Christians to make them shut up, because they never knew how to answer them. First, I would ask, "If God is just, and we are all created equal, then what about all the starving kids in Africa?" They usually answer with something stupid like, "God works in mysterious ways." That wasn't good enough.

Next I'd ask them, "If God treats us all the same, what about Oral Roberts and all of his money? That ain't right. He keeps getting richer and the poor just get poorer." Again, nobody knew how to answer. Especially in Tulsa. No one wanted to cross Oral Roberts.

So that's it, I thought. *I'll go in, have a cup of coffee, ask my two questions, and leave. I might stick around long enough to laugh at Danny and James, though.*

I backed into a parking space right next to James' Harley. I walked up the stairs and looked for apartment 205. I knocked on the door . . .

. . . and a beautiful lady answered it.

I said, "I'm sorry, I must have the wrong apartment. I'm looking for Jack."

She said, "Hi. I'm Fawnda, Jack's wife."

Well, I thought, *scratch "ugly women" off the list.* I walked in, and the first thing I noticed was that there weren't any Bibles on the tables. There were no crosses on the walls, and no plastic pictures of Jesus either.

I did see Jack, though, sitting at the kitchen table talking to Danny and James. He offered me the seat just to his left, where I sat and listened to him tell both Danny and James about Jesus. He really didn't talk to me all evening. He just talked to them about the love of Jesus.

The more he talked, the more confused I got. I had always known that Jesus loved the little children, but I grew up believing that once you become an adult, he was pissed at you. Turn or burn. The lake of fire. God's gonna french-fry you. Get saved, or go to hell. That was the only theology I had ever heard.

It didn't take long before I started feeling queasy inside, like my insides were all in the wrong place. I actually reached to feel my buck knife on my belt, just in case I needed it.

While talking about how Jesus loves us, Jack called his daughter in from the other room. "Jessica, come here a minute." A little five-year-old ran up to the table. She had pigtails and a yellow ribbon. She was cute.

Jack said, "Jessica, I want to introduce you to my friends. That guy over there is Danny Woodley. That other guy is James Hughes, and this big guy right beside me is John Swanger." Then he turned to us and said, "This is my daughter, Jessica." With that he said, "You can go back and play now, sweetheart."

Then he turned back to us and said "I am much bigger than her, and I am also more powerful. I could twist her arm behind her back and make her do anything I want. But that's not how our relationship is. I love that girl with my whole heart and she loves me with hers. She will do anything I want because she loves me, not because she's afraid of me. And that's how I am with Jesus. More accurately, that's how Jesus is with me. I follow and obey Him not because I am afraid of Him but because I love Him and He loves me."

Just then Fawnda walked to the table and set a large meatloaf and bowl of potatoes down. Then corn on the cob and cornbread muffins. "Time for a break from the preaching," she said.

Jack blessed the food and asked Jesus to guide the conversation for the remainder of the evening. Dinner was great and dessert was cherry pie.

As Fawnda was clearing the dishes, James spoke for the first time. "Excuse me, pastor, but if Jesus loves everyone and we are all created equal, what about all the starving kids in Africa?"

Jack answered, "Well, obviously, Jim, you have a heart for missions. We need to get you saved and into the mission field so you can go out there and feed them." I was shocked. Not only that James had asked my question, but that Jack had an answer.

Then, just like that, Danny spoke. "Jack, what about Oral Roberts and all his money? People keep getting poorer and he keeps getting richer. That ain't right."

"Do you think Oral Roberts is a hypocrite?" Jack asked.

Danny said, "You're damn right I do."

Jack responded, "So, you are saying there is a hypocrite standing between you and Jesus."

Danny said, "Exactly."

"You do realize that in order for the hypocrite to stand between you and Jesus, that means the hypocrite would have to be closer to Jesus than you are. You don't need Oral Roberts as an excuse to go to hell, and Oral Roberts can't get you into heaven. God will deal with Oral Roberts just like He will deal with you."

I thought, *Crap. I don't have any questions I can ask.* Most of my pre-conceived ideas of what a Christian was went out the window along with my two questions. Up to this point, the only Christians I had known were the older friends my grandmother attended church with, the blue-haired Baptists. Nice ladies, but I wouldn't want to marry one of them.

Just then, without warning, Jack turned to me. "So what are you going to do, John?"

I said, "To be honest, I'd like to go home and snort some coke, and read the Bible."

"Let me get you a Bible," Jack said, and jumped up.

I said, "You're not much of a preacher."

"Why?"

"Because if you were, you'd be telling me I have to quit doing coke or I'm going to hell."

Jack said, "That's not my job. It's my job to introduce you to Jesus. It's His job to change you."

If we had more preachers like that, I thought, *there'd be more people coming to Jesus.*

As Jack came back to the table with the Bible, James spoke up. "I want to go with John."

I don't know if he heard "cocaine" or "Bible" from what I'd said. But either way, we were heading to my house.

CHAPTER THIRTY-THREE

THE NIGHT

We left around 9:00 P.M. and stopped for gas about halfway home. James picked up a six-pack and shoved it in his saddlebags. Within fifteen minutes, we were dropping our kickstands and heading up the three short steps to the back door of my apartment.

I froze.

James said, "What's wrong?"

I answered, "I forgot. There's a girl in here."

He said, "How do you forget you have a girl living with you? And why didn't you say something?"

"I don't know, I just forgot. And I did say something. Just now."

So we did the manliest thing we could do. We reached behind and stuffed our Bibles under our belts. Then we zipped up our leathers and walked in.

I could see Brenda was asleep in the bedroom. I walked over and turned the TV off. Then I gently pulled the bedroom door closed and went to the bathroom. When I came back out, I could see that James had taken or smoked something really potent and was already passed out at the kitchen table, slobbering on his Bible.

I went to the freezer and retrieved my eight-ball. Brenda had snorted a couple of lines so it was just shy of full. I grabbed the mirror and a razor blade from the top of the fridge and sat in the recliner. I turned on the reading lamp and opened the Bible to Matthew.

I did a couple of lines and then started reading. I would stop every now and then to refresh my nose.

By 6:00 A.M. I had run out of coke, and I had read the entire New Testament. I decided it was time to have a talk with God. I said, not out loud, but in my mind, *How do I know this is real? How do I know it is this one, and not Islam or Buddhism? Or how about Hinduism? Or Mormonism or even atheism?*

As far as I know, some crazy guy could have written this out on toilet paper in prison. He hands it to a couple of inmates in the other cells, and they hand it to others, then next thing you know two billion people are believing something some crazy guy made up. Everything I read sounds good, but You need to prove to me You are real.

If You prove You are real, I'll quit doing coke. I'll quit drinking. I'll stop riding with the motorcycle clubs. I'll call Goodwill and have them come get all this hot stuff from my apartment. I'll quit working on the strip. I'll call my dealers and tell them they need to find another supplier. I'll call my wholesaler and tell him I am no longer buying any product. And I'll spend the rest if my life telling people about You."

I got up and put my Bible in the kitchen cabinet. I slid James' Bible from under his chin and placed it with mine. I sat back down in my recliner and looked at my watch. I said, once again in my heart, not out loud, *If I'm going to do this, that girl in there can't stay here. I don't want her hurt, and I don't want her mad. But if I do this, she has to go.*

I looked at my watch again, and said in my mind, *You have five minutes, God. I have to go to work.*

Just then the bedroom door opened and Brenda walked out. She looked at James passed out on the table, then she looked at me. "Why didn't you come to bed last night?" she asked.

I said, kind of mumbling, "I don't know. I was just hanging."

She said, "You got saved last night, didn't you?"

I said, "Yes. I guess I did."

She said, "I should leave then, shouldn't I?"

"Yes. I guess you should," I answered. With that, she picked up her little bag of G-strings and walked out the door. As the door closed, I heard God speak to me. Not in my heart like I spoke to Him, but out loud. I heard Him with my ears.

He said, "I did what you said. Now you do what you said."

I quickly looked at James to see if it was him talking. He was still out. I called Jack.

"Jack, I think I got saved."

He said, "Hold on. I'll be right there."

I woke up James and told him it was time to go home. He just went upstairs to Danny's apartment. As it turns out, they were cousins.

First thing I did was call Tiger. "I'm sorry, Tiger, but I can no longer work there. Thank you for the job. But it's time for me to move on."

She said, "I understand. Having a gun pulled on you can change a man."

I thought, *She has no clue. I didn't quit because of the gun.*

Then I called my dealers. I said to each of them, "I am no longer supplying coke. You will have to find another source."

Without fail, they each said, "Tell me who your supplier is so I can buy directly from him." I refused and they were all pissed. Then I called my supplier/mechanic. I said, "Mark, I am no longer in the business. I quit."

He wanted to know who my dealers were. "You can't leave me hanging like this," he said. "John, you are pissing a lot of people off who were counting on you."

I just said, "Mark, I'm out." And I hung up.

I called Budd and told him what happened. "Budd, I became a Christian last night. I can't hang around anymore."

He said, "John, we need you. Every chapter has a chaplain; we don't yet. You could be ours."

I said, "I don't even know what I'm doing yet. I have no clue how to be a chaplain."

He said, "Keep in touch, John."

CHAPTER THIRTY-FOUR

A NEW MORNING

It was a quarter to seven when Jack pulled up. I was loading some clothes and my guitar into my MG. "I'm calling Goodwill to come empty out my place, and I'll be looking for somewhere to stay."

He asked, "Why?"

"I just pissed off a few dealers as well as my supplier. I need to disappear for a bit."

Jack said, "Fawnda and I are headed to school, but you can go hang out at our place, at least until we get home." He handed me a key and they drove off.

I called Goodwill and told them the key would be under the floor mat by the back door. I said they could have everything in the apartment, and no, I did not need a receipt.

I put the key under the mat and drove off, leaving my old life behind.

I carried my guitar up the stairs to Jack and Fawnda's, and walked back into apartment 205 to begin my new journey. I tried to lay down on the couch but couldn't sleep. Finally I sat up and opened my guitar case. I grabbed a pen and paper from the kitchen table and sat back down.

I Believe

VERSE 1
I believe, believe with all my heart.
Because I believe, I've got a brand new start.
I believe, I'm newborn today.

No need to hide, I won't hide my face.
When I repent, I receive His grace.
Now in His name, my sins are washed away.

CHORUS
A new creation, In His holy name.
Now I'm anew, I'm no longer the same,
For at the cross old things passed away.
A new power, that I needed the most.
Yeah, every hour with the Holy Ghost.
So now I walk with Him day to day.

VERSE 2
When He died, He died for me.
When He arose, He set me free.
He took my place and gave many gifts to men.
Now He sits upon His heavenly throne,
And I believe in His name alone.
He lives in me, and I believe in Him.

Written Wednesday, February 2, 1983
John Swanger, © 1983

I played my new song several times. Finally I lay back down on the couch and fell asleep.

Jack woke me up at almost 2:00 P.M. I was excited and asked if I could play my new song for him and Fawnda. They sat down and I played.

Jack pulled out his Bible and started showing me how Jesus was actually talked about throughout the entire Bible, including the Old Testament. He showed me scriptures all the way from Genesis through Revelation. "Perhaps there is a song somewhere in there for you," he said.

Fawnda made us some breakfast, including homemade biscuits. I was really hungry, and they were great.

Jack started talking to me about my past. He knew I'd been in prison for bank robbery, but he wanted to know more about me. Like why I had robbed banks, and what did I think led me to a life of crime?

I told him about my time with Dr. Bliss, the prison psychiatrist, and how she concluded I was trying to buy my mother's love and needed to accept the fact that my mother didn't love me and probably never would. I told him Barb said that accepting it as fact would allow for my healing, so I could move on with my life a much healthier man.

Jack said, "Accepting the fact that she doesn't love you is just the first step. Now that you have Jesus in you to help you, you need to find it in your heart to forgive her for not loving you."

I said, "I don't know how to do that. I've just put it out of my mind. I never think about it."

He said, "We can pray, and you can give it to the Lord. Ask Him to put forgiveness in your heart."

I said, "I want to do that."

Jack and I prayed, and Fawnda joined in. We all asked God to show me a better way to live, a life not filled with hurt and unforgiveness.

Jack said, "You might want to get some more sleep, John. We have a long evening ahead."

I lay back down on the couch and fell right off into a dream. In it, I was walking through a heavy fog in the middle of nowhere. The fog was so thick I couldn't even see my feet. I looked ahead and saw Jesus walking toward me. His hands were reaching out for me. Just as I grabbed for His hand, I saw that I was actually in the clouds. I couldn't see the ground because there was no ground. As Jesus reached for my hand, I felt I was going to fall but He caught me. Suddenly I felt safe.

Fawnda woke me at six in the evening. "You'd better get ready," she said. "We will be leaving in about fifteen minutes."

"Where are we going?" I asked.

"It's Wednesday, John. We are going to church," she answered, just as Jack walked in.

I said to him, "I thought you worked on Wednesdays."

He answered, "I do. But I took vacation this week."

We drove to Broken Arrow and entered a huge church. There was a massive Bible on a pedestal in the entryway. The Bible was open, with Mark 11:23-24 highlighted:

> *For verily I say unto you, That whosoever shall say unto this mountain, Be thou removed, and be thou cast into the sea; and shall not doubt in his heart, but shall believe that those things which he saith shall come to pass; he shall have whatsoever he*

saith. Therefore I say unto you, whatsoever things ye desire, when
ye pray, believe that ye receive them, and ye shall have them.

We walked into the sanctuary and took some seats up high on the last row. An older man with a pinstripe suit walked to the pulpit and began talking about something I had never heard from my grandmother's church. He spoke about how we can claim anything we desire if we call upon the name of the Lord.

"But you can't pray for Cadillacs on doughnut faith," he said. "First you have to believe enough to receive a doughnut. Then work your way up to a Coupe De Ville."

I sat there waiting for something, and I didn't know what. I was hungry for God and for everything that meant.

I leaned over and said to Jack, "I don't just want the chicken soup, I want the whole chicken."

Jack replied, "You have accepted Jesus into your heart. Now you need to go forward and make a public profession of your faith."

I got up and started to walk down the stairs. Jack caught my arm. "Not yet, Tiger. You have to wait until he calls you down."

"Who is that guy?" I asked.

"That is Kenneth Hagin."

Rev. Hagin asked for people to come forward. "Now," Jack said.

I headed down and ended up standing in a line that stretched across the front of the stage. I was the last one on the left of the stage, and Rev. Hagin started at the other end. "You are all here to ask God to forgive you for your sins," he said. "First you need to forgive those who have wronged you and fill your hearts with forgiveness towards others. Because Matthew 6:14-15 says to forgive others so God can forgive you for your sins."

One by one, he made his way down the line coming toward me. He would stop and lay his hands on each person and pray something. Over and over, until he was finally in front of me. I was standing there in my leathers with my long hair and my chains and buck knife hanging from my belt. I was in a sleeveless shirt, my tattoos showing. Then Rev. Hagin simply tapped me on the shoulder and turned to walk away.

I said, "Hey, old man." He turned back to me. "I want what you gave all of them."

He said, "Son, they came to get what you've already got."

Then he announced to the crowd, "We have counselors who are going to take you all to our Upper Room. They will lay hands on you all, and you will receive the Holy Spirit."

An old man walked up and took me by the arm. He told me his name was Richard Halverson. I thought, *I don't know who this guy is, but I want to talk to Jack.* I was getting really agitated. Just then Jack came and replaced the old man on my arm.

He said, "John, I should have told you about this. It is a good thing, just roll with it. I'm sure you read about it last night."

I said, "I read something about being filled with the Holy Spirit, but I didn't understand it."

"Do you trust me, John?" Jack asked.

"Yes," I said.

We got to the Upper Room and they lined us all up in two rows facing a man in the front. He looked at us and said, "We are going to lay hands on each of you, and when we do you will all be filled with the Holy Spirit and begin speaking in tongues." He snapped his fingers and added, "Just like that."

Instantly, I fell on my knees and heard myself speaking in some kind of a language I had never heard. It just kept going.

I stepped back and sat on a small riser built for a choir to practice on. I began weeping. Suddenly I felt the burden of all I had done in my life being lifted. I felt as if God was taking the fall for my crimes, and I was walking away a free man. I couldn't stop crying, and I couldn't stop speaking in tongues.

Suddenly, I felt a rush that would dwarf any rush I had ever felt from drugs. I couldn't begin to express how thankful I was that God had forgiven me.

After some time, I finally was able to return to the natural world around me. Jack was right there. He said, "Let's go home."

We got back to their apartment, and Jack started explaining to me what had just happened. He was flipping back and forth in the Bible and reading verses to me. All I knew was that I was at peace for the first time in my life. I really didn't know what it was, but I knew it was from God and I was okay with it.

Fawnda asked me to play my new song again, and I did. Then I felt inspiration and asked for more paper and the pen. I was thinking about

all the scriptures Jack had shown me earlier about Jesus being in the Old
Testament and the New, and I wrote:

Emmanuel

VERSE 1

Foxes got their holes, and the birds they got their nests
You know the Son of Man, He ain't got no place to rest
Rejected of us all, despised among all man
Acquainted with all kinds of grief, we hid our face from Him.

CHORUS
Emmanuel, Emmanuel

VERSE 2

Taken from the prison, and cut off of the land
For the sins of my people, He is the great I Am
He made His grave with the wicked, with the rich in His death
He had done no violence, deceit not in His breath.

CHORUS
Emmanuel, Emmanuel

VERSE 3

Dressed in a robe of purple, with thorns upon His head.
Hail the King of the Jews, beat 'til He was half dead.
The blood and water flowed, down from His side.
See the man from Nazareth, the man they crucified.

CHORUS
Emmanuel, Emmanuel

VERSE 4

Death could not hold Him, He overcame the grave.
He gave His life unselfishly for all mankind to save.
I Am the great Messiah and all mankind must hear,
I hold the keys to death and hell. My return is near.

CHORUS
Emmanuel, Emmanuel

VERSE 5
Behold, I come quickly. My reward is with me.
Give to every man according, as his work shall be.
I Am the Alpha and Omega, the Beginning and the End.
The First and the Last, and I shall return again.

CHORUS
Emmanuel, Emmanuel

Written Wednesday, February 2, 1983
John Swanger, © 1983

Two songs in one day. I thought, *Something strange is going on.* I had previously written only two other songs, and one of them had taken me six months to write. *This has to be a God thing.*

Jack said, "Hey, you old drug dealer. Looks like you just might have yourself a new vocation."

CHAPTER THIRTY-FIVE

FOLLOWING GOD NOW

Thursday, February 3, 1983

The next day, after Jack and Fawnda returned from school, they spent a couple of hours teaching me about Jesus. Then he said he needed to prepare his sermon for that evening. "John, you and I are going to the Oklahoma State Penitentiary in McAlester to talk to the guys on death row. I will be preaching and you can sing your songs."

While Jack worked, Fawnda talked to me about prayer and how I needed to pray all the time. "You have a pipeline to God," she said. "He will direct you if you trust Him and lean on Him."

We got to the prison, and met a handful of other people there. I got a bit nervous. We walked to the gate, and the guard just stuck out a basket. We all dropped our driver's licenses in, and he opened the gate to let us walk in.

Jack spoke and said that no matter what we have done, Jesus wants to forgive us. We can go to Heaven if we accept Jesus as Lord. I sang "I Believe," and then I sang "Emmanuel." They applauded.

On the way back to the apartment, I realized that I hadn't had any cocaine or alcohol, and yet I wasn't going through withdrawals. No palpitating heartbeats, no blood pressure tanking, and no DTs. I had no desire to drink or to do coke. It was like I had never been addicted in the first place. I realized that God had delivered me from my cocaine addiction as well my alcoholism. I was blessed.

For the next few weeks I would sleep on Jack and Fawnda's couch while they were at school. Then Fawnda would teach me in the afternoon while Jack slept. Then I would go to work with Jack while Fawnda slept at night. Then in the morning we would do it all over again. This went on for a couple of months. Finally an apartment opened up in the same building and I rented it.

After just three times going into McAlester prison, they changed the policies and started doing background checks on all volunteers. Needless to say, I was denied re-entry.

Over the next few weeks I wrote several new songs. However I began to lose faith in Jack. I had erroneously put him on a pedestal.

Jack was constantly bickering with Fawnda. My natural instinct to protect women was clashing with my newfound faith in Jack. One day Jack said he wanted to go riding with me.

I said, "You don't have a motorcycle."

He asked if I could borrow my brother David's bike so we could ride around a bit. I called David, and he said he didn't mind as long as I was the one riding his bike. We got ready to go pick up David's bike, and I started having a queasy feeling, like I knew we shouldn't go. Jack sat on my bike and offered me the passenger seat. I sat down but really wanted to back out. I looked at Fawnda and could clearly see she was feeling the same thing. I really felt like the Holy Spirit was telling me to not go. However my love and appreciation for Jack was telling me, *Who am I to question Jack? After all, He hears God better than anyone I've ever met.* I was afraid, but I trusted Jack's judgment.

Halfway there I was praying in the spirit, and I looked at my hands. All of a sudden I knew we were going to have a wreck. I thought about how I needed my hands for playing my guitar, so I pulled my leather gloves on. "Jack," I said, "I think we should slow down."

He said, "We're fine, John. I know what I'm doing."

We were on a two-lane blacktop. Suddenly I heard a bit of chain noise and said, "Jack, the chain is clanging." I barely got the words out of my mouth when the chain broke and the back wheel locked up.

We started fishtailing. The rear of the bike swayed to the left, and when it went back it left me in the other lane, sliding along in a sitting up position. I looked at my hands and saw that somehow the gloves were missing. I looked ahead and saw a big black van heading right at me. I cried out, "God, make that van stop!"

He did. I saw the tires smoking as it slid to a stop.

Then I cried out, "Now make me stop, God!"

As I slid to a stop, I turned to my right to see Jack sliding up to stop right next to me. I said, "What took you so long?"

He said, "I was carrying your motorcycle. But as soon as I managed to dump it, I started to gain on you."

Just then the lady in the black van opened the door and stepped out. She said, "Are you two all right?"

"Yes ma'am," we said.

"Well, why?" she asked.

Jack answered, "The Holy Spirit, ma'am."

I stood up and took inventory of myself. I had a small raspberry on my right elbow and another on the left cheek of my butt. Other than that, I was okay. I saw that my wallet and checkbook were missing. I walked back up the road and gathered them, along with my gloves. A man offered to haul my motorcycle and us on over to David's house.

Once we were there I asked David if he had a Bible. He had an old family Bible, the kind no one reads but that looks good on the end table. I opened it randomly and looked at the verse my fingers landed on. It was Psalm 91:11-12:

"For he shall give his angels charge over thee, to keep thee in all thy ways. They shall bear thee up in their hands, lest thou dash thy foot against a stone."

I took off for Dallas to visit my family and let them know what had happened in my life. There was a family reunion planned and it seemed like good timing. I felt great about the changes I had started and wanted to share my new faith with them. That day, I put on my favorite Jesus t-shirt. It said, "The next time the devil reminds you of your past, remind him of his future." It also had Revelation 12:12 on it: "Therefore rejoice, you heavens and you who dwell in them! But woe to the earth and the sea, because the devil has gone down to you! He is filled with fury, because he knows that his time is short."

I showed up at Nanny's house for the family reunion. Everyone was there. I saw Nanny as I walked through the door and went over to her immediately to tell her I accepted Jesus into my life. "I am overjoyed," she said. "John, I have prayed for this day ever since you got arrested."

I told her, "Thank you, Nanny. I love you."

She asked, "Do you remember when I took you and David to see Billy Graham when you were seven and David was six?"

"Yes, I do."

"Do you remember that he baptized you and David?"

I answered, "Yes, but it didn't mean anything to me then. It does now."

She said, "Perhaps not, but I know it meant something to God. Why do you think He protected you through all you have done and been through?"

"I guess we'll find out," I said.

I talked to several of my relatives and was surprised to feel they were skeptical. But Walt was the worst. "Hey, John," he said, "What's the scam?"

I asked, "What do you mean?"

"What are you trying to pull over on your grandmother with this Jesus shirt and all?"

"No scam, Walt. I am a Christian now."

"Yeah, right."

I left there brokenhearted. I thought I was the black sheep of the family before Jesus, but Walt had made me feel even more of a black sheep. The drive back to Tulsa gave me time to think. I concluded that I perhaps deserved the skeptics. I had been a criminal for thirty years and a believer for only a couple of months. It just made me more determined to become closer to what God created me to be.

When I got back to Tulsa, I stood on my bed and began praying. I asked, "God, how do I know I am really following You and not just playing a game?"

God's answer came quick and was simple: "Who is there with you right now?"

I answered, "No one."

"Then there is no one to fool. It's just you and Me, John. Trust me, it's real."

CHAPTER THIRTY-SIX

TRUSTING THE LORD

"It is better to trust in the LORD than to have confidence in man."
Psalm 118:8

The motorcycle accident got me thinking about other things that I was not really in agreement with Jack about. The whole "name it and claim it" theology, which was a big part of his world, was totally counter to my own personal faith. I was busy trying to serve God and it felt like that theology was self-serving. It seemed to me the idea should be closer to what John F. Kennedy said, more like, "Ask not what God can do for you, ask what you can do for God."

I thought of Matthew 6:33, which said, "Seek ye first the kingdom of God, and his righteousness; and all these things shall be added unto you." I kept feeling that the Christians I knew were seeking the things instead of seeking God. The more I drew closer to God, the less I wanted anything outside of God. My desires for stuff began to fade. All I wanted was God—and a wife.

This search brought even more dissatisfaction with the believers I'd become acquainted with. Jack introduced me to a couple of Christian girls, but both dates ended badly. It felt to me like it was no different than just being in the world. I just wanted God to send me a wife, and they had other things on their minds. I decided I wouldn't date, because it obviously wasn't working out.

I hauled my motorcycle back from David's house, and Budd said he would humble himself and fix it for me, even though it wasn't a "real" motorcycle. When he had it back together, he offered me a deal when I went to pick it up. "I have an old pan head that I just finished rebuilding, and I would like to make you a trade."

I said, "I can't ride with you guys."

Budd said, "I want you to have the pan even if you can't hang with us. But I want your MG and your rice burner."

I took the deal and brought my titles to him the next day. He signed over the Pan and we were both happy. I asked him, "Why would you want the burner though, Budd?"

He answered, "Come by tomorrow and you'll see."

The next day I showed up at Tulsa Harley Davidson in time to watch bikers, mostly Mongols, paying a dollar a swing to pulverize my Honda Chopper with a sledgehammer in the parking lot. It looked terrible. It was literally being pounded into the pavement.

Chief said, "Thanks, John. We've already made more than you would believe. At a dollar a swing."

Budd said, "I think we'll keep it in the parking lot for therapy." I had a hard time laughing about it, but I did try to smile. Finally owning my first Harley helped a bit.

Two months later Jack and Fawnda graduated from Rhema. They asked me if I wanted to move with them to Denver, Colorado. Jack said, "I plan to open a church, and I want you to lead worship."

Despite our differences, I said yes, and helped them pack. Then I bought a 1967 GMC pickup truck. I paid just over $600 for it.

James came by one evening and told me his Harley had caught fire. "I was heading to the Harley Davidson shop and flames started coming out of the exhaust manifold. I barely got stopped before it went up."

I asked, "Are you okay?"

He answered, "I got a small burn on my calf, just above the boot. But no, I'm not okay. I lost my scoot, bro." It was a total loss. He was heartbroken.

I decided to give him my pan. He was blown away. He said, "No one has ever done anything that nice for me."

I felt like it was what God wanted me to do.

Within two days, Jack, Fawnda, little Jessica, and I were on the road to Denver.

CHAPTER THIRTY-SEVEN

DISENCHANTMENT

The trip was difficult. I slept in the back seat of the car, as did Jessica. Along the way, Jack kept yelling and occasionally cussing at Fawnda. She was crying. I just lay there and acted like I was asleep. I gently snuck my hand up on to Fawnda's right shoulder just to let her know I was praying for her. I was careful not to let Jack see.

I told myself Jack was just under a lot of stress, and I hoped things would get better. I could never understand why, in times of struggle, people lash out at the person who loves them the most.

We got to Denver and went to stay with a couple named Rick and Cathy in a geodesic dome house up near Morrison that Rick had built. He owned a custom-cabinet shop called Mountain States Cabinets, and he hired me right away. I started working there the next morning.

Rick had a sister named Gail who ran a barbershop with her friend Marcia. They agreed to let Jack, Fawnda, and me hold church services there every Sunday evening until Jack could find a suitable building for a permanent home.

A month later, Jack located an old church building in Englewood. There, we opened Family Faith Center. Jack preached and I led worship. The church was growing but I was becoming less and less a fan of Christians. I was trying to stay away from the women in the church. Two actually came to me separately and basically threw themselves at me. One said to me, "God said to me that I am to leave my husband. I am to become your Sarah and you are to become my Abraham." Yeah, right.

I was also becoming less supportive of Jack. He was a gifted speaker, but I couldn't understand why God would anoint and use such a man.

I watched him step down from the pulpit, go to the back room, and tell some of the vilest and horrendous jokes I had ever heard. *How can he be so gifted and at the same time be so mean to Fawnda and me?* I wondered.

I, along with a few others, left and started attending church in Littleton at a place called Family Worship Center. But I still struggled. the part of me I hated the most was being phony, acting like I was something I wasn't. I could live with being rejected, with not feeling like I had a family, and with being a bank robber. But I hated being a hypocrite. That was the thing I wanted to change the most while I was in prison. I never again wanted to act one way around a person and another way when I was not around that person. But here I was, living a secret life, and acting like a Christian at church. I was no better than Jack. I had become the hypocrite I despised.

I called my new pastor, Mark, and asked him if we could meet for breakfast. He said he happened to have that day open so we met at a Denny's just up the road from where I was staying.

February 26, 1984

I walked into the Denny's ten minutes early, as was my habit for all meetings. More of a defense than a courtesy. I always tried to find a seat where I could clearly see the door and have no one sitting behind me—a habit I developed while in prison.

Mark entered and took the seat across the table from me. Right away he reached into his jacket and pulled out a small box of business cards. But instead of typical business cards, they were scripture cards. Each one was different. He just reached into the center and randomly pulled one out and handed it to me. It read:

"Then you will call, and the LORD will answer; you will cry for help, and he will say: 'Here am I.'" (Isaiah 58:9) I stuck it in my pocket.

Mark asked, "What's up, John?"

I cut right to the chase. "I am going to go back to Dallas where I am from. I'm going to go backslide."

"Any particular reason?" he asked.

"I feel like I have become a hypocrite. So if I am going to sin, I am at least going to be honest about it. No more pretending I am something I am not."

Mark asked, "Do you expect you will ever return to God? And if so, when?"

I said, "I am guessing I will be back here in six months or so. I just need to get my bearings and get this out of my system."

Then he asked, "Did you call me to breakfast to talk you out of this?"

I answered, "No, not at all."

He concluded, "Okay, then. Let's order."

We had a big breakfast including bacon and pancakes. After we had finished Mark asked about the card he had handed me. "What verse did you get?"

I asked, "You don't know?"

He said, "No, I just pulled a random one from the box."

I read the card to him and he lit up. "Sounds pretty pertinent, don't you think?"

"I guess so."

He said, "He will be waiting for your call."

I went home, loaded my things into my pickup truck, and hit the road. It was noon by the time I drove up the on-ramp of I-25 south. The light rain had built momentum until it transformed into a full-fledged thunderstorm. It didn't lighten up until I crossed the city limit sign in Lamar. I pulled up to the pumps at a combination service station and restaurant, a place called Mo's BBQ. It was owned by an old guy named Willard who served BBQ and authentic Mexican food. He saw me driving up and noticed my guitar standing in the passenger seat of my truck. "Are you any good at that thing?" he asked.

I said, "That thing made me a pretty good living for several years."

He followed me inside and sat down at my table. "Where you heading?" he asked.

I answered, "Dallas."

"You in a hurry?"

"Not really. Why?"

"If you wouldn't mind doing a few songs for my customers this evening, I'll give you a few bucks, all you can eat of the best damned BBQ this side of Terlingua, and a warm, dry bed for the night," he offered.

I'm not sure if it was the smell of the BBQ or the chance to get back on stage that tempted me, but either way, I accepted.

"Pull your truck to the side of the building alongside the smoker. Come back inside, and I'll dish you up a plate," he said.

He was right; it was the best BBQ I have, to this day, ever had. There wasn't a stage but he moved one of the tables away from the corner of the room and then adjusted a couple of ceiling lights that were illuminating velvet paintings on the walls to form makeshift stage lights. He also sat his cowboy hat on the floor in front of the "stage" and threw a couple of fives into it.

At closing time, Willard took a fifty-dollar bill out of the register and handed it to me. He also emptied the hat into my guitar case. All totaled, I made about a $125. He showed me to the back room where there was a twin-size bed and a shower. I enjoyed both.

I woke to the smell of bacon.

Willard said, "Over easy okay with you?"

"Yes," I answered.

"I can't keep you on permanent, but if you want to hang out a few more days I'll do the same deal we had last night," he said.

I ended up staying there three nights. Then it was time to go. I drove the remaining six hundred miles straight through to Dallas. As I crossed into Dallas, I stopped at a pay phone and called my mom.

"What are you doing?" she asked. "Just here for a visit?"

"Mom, I'd like to stay a while if it's okay with you," I said.

"Johnny, there's always room for you."

"I should be there in about a half hour."

I was tired and wanted to sleep by the time I got there, but Walt asked me to go with him to pick up a couple of cars. I was impressed by Walt's new wrecker. He had a new three-quarter-ton Chevy with a custom 440 Holmes bed along with dollies. We found the first car right away. Walt drove to the repo lot and we dropped it. Then we drove to the main parking lot of Texas Instruments and started combing through each row.

I asked, "Where is the repo order for this one?"

He said, "I left it at home. But don't worry. Just keep your eyes out for a 1983 Dodge Ram."

"What color?" I asked.

"John. Don't worry about it." he said.

Halfway down the next row he spotted a charcoal grey Ram. Without checking the license plate or the serial number, he just whipped around and backed under it. We jumped out and put the hooks on it and were rolling as I pressed the PTO to lift the pickup on the sling. We took it to another parking lot near where the owner of Allstate Adjusters lived, the repo company Walt worked for.

We stopped at Mid-Continent Truck Stop for coffee, and Walt pulled out his wallet.

He handed me a fifty and said, "This is for the first car we got tonight." Then he handed me three hundred more and said, "This is for the Ram."

It was past three in the morning by the time I got to bed.

CHAPTER THIRTY-EIGHT

DANCING WITH THE DEVIL

By the next afternoon I was once again sitting with Walt at the truck stop, sipping coffee. He said, "It's good to see you've gotten over that Jesus thing you were sporting there for awhile."

"I haven't gotten over anything. I just wanted to come see you and Mom," I said.

"Yeah, right. Whatever you say, John."

"Not everything is as cut and dry as you like to think, Walt."

"There's black. And then there's white. You were black, then white, now you are black again. That's all there is to it."

I had a hard time arguing with him. I had just walked away from my life as a Christian. Not to mention I helped him steal a pickup truck the night before.

"Do you know what a deer lease is?" Walt asked.

I answered, "No."

"It's where deer hunters pay ranchers money to be able to hunt deer on their land. They make deals so they can come out and stay three to four weeks during hunting season and even park their luxury 35-foot camping trailers there all year long so they don't have to haul them there and back each year."

"What does that have to do with us?" I asked.

"These trailers cost about thirty to forty thousand dollars each. I have a deal with some of the guys where I bring them a trailer and set it on the deer lease at their campsite, and they pay me four thousand for each one I deliver," he said.

"And?" I asked.

"And, I need your help," Walt said. "You showed me last night that you're back in the game, and I know I can trust you to help me make things happen."

We started stealing a trailer every three weeks or so. And Walt, for the first time in my life, was actually paying me what he said he would. Each trailer brought me two thousand cash. I started going to Las Vegas as soon as I got paid. Walt would drive me to Irving and drop me at DFW airport, and I would fly to Vegas. After blowing my cash, I would hitchhike back to Dallas, team up with Walt, and then do it again.

Walt and I repossessed a Harley Davidson in Irving. It was for a bank in Colorado Springs. They paid Walt two hundred for the repo and said they would give me $500 to transport it back to Colorado, along with a return ticket to Dallas. I took off, and stopped along the way in Lamar, where I visited my friend Willard. He remembered me from my trip down and asked if I had my guitar with me.

I answered, "I am on a motorcycle. So, no."

He said, "Well, either way, friend, your dinner is on me. And you are welcome to stay in the back for the night." I was glad, because I had just a few dollars on me until I hit Colorado Springs and could collect for the Harley. I took off the next morning.

When I got back to Texas, Walt and I were driving around in Fort Worth one afternoon repo'ing cars and looking for a Caddy. Walt spotted a beautiful black 1967 GMC step-side pickup, totally restored. Custom seats and tinted windows. Mag wheels and wide tires.

"You want it?" he asked.

I answered, "I suppose so." We hooked it up and hauled it home. We removed the serial number plates from the doors and replaced them with the ones from my old beater. Then we drove both trucks to a junk yard where Walt knew the boss. Walt had him weld a small bracket onto the side of the engine, just over the serial number stamped into the engine block, so it looked like it held some accessory. In exchange, we gave him my old beater truck.

Walt called it the "radiator cap repair job." You just take off the radiator cap and drive another truck under it.

The following week Walt and I went to Vegas together. We blew our two thousand each and then sold my newly restored pickup for fifteen hundred. Then we promptly blew that also. Walt called a friend to wire him some cash to fly back to Dallas. I hitchhiked back.

In all, I made seven trips to Vegas in six months. Just before the last trip, I went out with my siblings and uncles to play Bingo. The Texas Bingo Hall was open evenings and called ten games, each with a five-hundred-dollar payout. By the time the evening was over, my Uncle John was mad because I won two of the ten outright and split another with someone else. Then I won the fifty-dollar drawing for the door prize. I left there with thirteen hundred plus the two thousand I had received from Walt the night before. Instead of flying, I decided to hitch to Vegas so I could have more cash for the blackjack tables.

Mom packed my suitcase and threw in some chips and snacks for the trip. I always loved Heath bars and Skor. Toffee is the best thing ever invented, except of course Mom's dark chocolate walnut fudge, which she tucked a bag of beneath my clothes as a surprise.

Walt took me to the interstate and dropped me at a busy on ramp. As I got out of the truck, he said, "See you in about a week? We have orders to fill."

I answered, "We'll see. I might just hit it big this time and buy a house in Hawaii or something."

I made it to Vegas in two days, thanks to long rides and friendly people who didn't mind me sleeping as they drove. Quite often, drivers pick you up for the conversation to help them stay awake. But this time was different.

Somehow I managed to go through all my cash by the end of the first day. I ended up sleeping in an alley for several nights. I would also stand in line at the Keno windows in Harrah's on the south strip, acting like I was buying tickets, so I could get the free appetizers they came around handing out. They would also hand out tickets for the buffet. I asked the Keno runner, "Can I get one of those buffet tickets?"

"Sure," she said, "let me see your current Keno ticket." I showed her the worthless ticket I had grabbed off of a table that someone else had abandoned after their failed attempt at riches. Then she noticed my beat-up suitcase.

She said, "You need a current ticket. So if you wouldn't mind stepping up to the window and purchasing one, I'd be happy to give you a buffet pass."

Since I had no money to buy a Keno ticket, she asked me to leave. Before I could even pick up my jacket and suitcase, two security guards appeared and stood on either side of me. They grabbed my arms and my things, escorted me through the doors, and shoved me away. They tossed my suitcase at me and headed back in.

I decided it was time to head back to Dallas.

CHAPTER THIRTY-NINE

EASTWARD JOURNEY

Tuesday, August 21, 1984

The five-and-a-half-mile walk over to Interstate 515 took me a couple of hours. But then I got a ride before I even sat my things down. The man told me he was just heading to Henderson, Nevada. "But," he added, "I'm guessing that, like me, you can't wait to get out of this hell hole."

I answered, "Las Vegas hasn't been too good to me."

"Tell me about it," he said. "I just dropped 5K here. I'm thinking Henderson might bring me some luck. And it will be a better place for you to hitch a ride."

It only took twenty minutes for the fifteen miles to Henderson. I was pleased to be on my way back to Dallas. It was hot but it was also raining. As soon as he dropped me and parked his car to go spend more money, I stuck my thumb out. I stood on the shoulder of the highway for nearly an hour with not even a chance of getting a ride. Behind me was a parking lot and across the road was a large casino. A security truck with two armed guards pulled up. One of them addressed me: "You need to move on."

I answered, "I'm not on the casino's property."

The other said, "Move on or go to jail."

I took that as a sign that Nevada was no longer my friend. I began walking. Just then, a man came out of the casino and approached me as he crossed the street.

He said, "If you are heading east, I could use the company."

I climbed into his semi, and we took off. Just as we were out of sight from the casino he pulled the truck over. He got out and walked around the truck to my door. I thought he was going to tell me to get out but instead he asked, "Can you drive this thing?"

I answered, "It's been a while, but yes."

As I climbed into the driver's seat, he called out from the sleeper, "There is a truck stop in Flagstaff called Little America. Pull over there, and I'll take over. I'm going to get some sleep."

I took off and for the next four and a half hours, I was a truck driver. I pulled into Little America and called back to the sleeper. "Hey, sir. We are in Flagstaff."

He got out, walked to the coffee shop, and returned with two cups of coffee. "Thanks for the break," he said. "I really needed it. But this here is the end for you. Good luck."

I thanked him, and just as I took my suitcase out of the cab of the truck, a car pulled up and the driver rolled down his window. "You heading to New Mexico?"

I said, "Yes, sir, I am."

"Hop in. I can get you as far as Gallup, but let's stop in here and eat something first."

I said, "I don't have any money."

He said, "It's on me."

I was really hungry so the gesture was greatly appreciated. A half hour later we were on the road. The sun was going down when we pulled into the Navajo Travel Plaza in Gallup. The man said, "I don't have time for dinner, but I want to make sure you eat." He handed me ten dollars and drove off.

I went in and had an evening breakfast of biscuits and gravy with bacon and coffee. I had just enough left to buy a pack of Camels. I headed for the door and a couple who had been eating at the table next to mine offered me a ride. "If you are heading east, you can ride with us. I don't usually pick up hitchhikers when I have my wife with me, but you look pretty harmless."

I told him, "Thank you."

It was about midnight when I woke up. We were pulling off to the side of the road. The man said, "It's raining, so I thought I'd drop you here under this bridge so you can stay dry. Good luck to you. This is where we live."

I said, "Goodbye and thanks so much for the ride."

CHAPTER FORTY

DIVINE DETOUR

Thursday, August 23, 1984, Just Past Midnight

I sat my suitcase down and stuck my thumb out. Nothing. The rain was pounding, and I had to move a few times as it would run under the bridge and drip on me. I was hungry.

I was frustrated and decided to climb up under the overhang and sleep. I opened my suitcase and pulled on a couple of shirts over the one I was already wearing. I rolled up another to use as a pillow. It was really cold.

Morning came and I got up, sore and wet. It was hot but still raining. I just sat there and shook my head. Finally, I pulled off the extra clothes and repacked them into my suitcase. I carefully walked down the incline back to level ground, and stuck my thumb out again.

It was noon. I tried not to smoke away all my cigarettes, but I found myself lighting one right after another.

Nothing changed.

In all, I was under that bridge for two and a half days. Still cold at night, hot during the day. Broke, hungry, and now, out of cigarettes. I was pissed. By noon of the 25th, I was thinking I couldn't take it anymore.

I yelled out, "God, what am I doing wrong?" I wasn't looking for nor expecting an answer. It wasn't really a question. More of a frustration.

But I faintly heard, "You are going the wrong way."

I sat down, opened my suitcase, and took out my map. I looked it over and traced the bright yellow highlighter line I'd drawn from Las Vegas to Dallas. I shoved the map back into my suitcase and slammed it close. As I flipped the latches I thought *Well, that couldn't be God. I know what I'm doing.*

An hour passed. I spontaneously cried out again, "God, what am I doing wrong?"

Once again He answered. This time in a much louder voice. "You, John, are going the wrong way."

Again I opened my suitcase and pulled out my map. As my eyes and fingers followed the yellow line from Vegas, I caught sight of I-25, then Denver came into focus.

I had just started to argue with God when He prompted me to open my suitcase again. I did and spotted my Bible sticking up from the corner along the back wall. I didn't remember putting it in there, and it wasn't like my mom to pack it for me. I opened it up and found a note from Mom.

"Johnny," it said, "I hope you can find a way to go back to Denver. We both know Walt isn't good for you. I am afraid that you will end up back in prison if you keep hanging out with Walt. I love you, Mom."

I then flipped to the back cover and found the card Mark had given me.

> *"Then you will call, and the LORD will answer;*
> *you will cry for help, and he will say: Here am I."*
> Isaiah 58:9

On the corner of it, I had written February 26, 1984. I climbed up the embankment to look at the interstate on top of it, and found the overpass was indeed I-25. Before I sat my suitcase down, a car pulled up and the driver offered me a ride. I thanked him and told him I was heading to Denver. I added, "But if you don't mind, I'd like to just go to the nearest restaurant so I can try and get something to eat."

He took the first exit and dropped me at a small, family-owned hamburger joint. I walked in and saw an older lady behind the counter. "Excuse me ma'am," I said, "I was wondering if you had any work I could do in exchange for something to eat?"

She said, "There is no work, but I will feed you. Have a seat."

I replied, "No ma'am. I'm not a bum. I'm just a man who is trying to find my way back to Jesus. So if you don't mind, I'd just as soon work for the meal."

She said, "Okay, if you insist. You can wash the windows in the kitchen, but sit down and eat first."

She brought me a chocolate shake and put in an order for a double cheeseburger with fries. I finished it and stood up. "Do you have window cleaning gear?" I asked, "I'll get started."

She said, "There are no windows in the kitchen."

Just then a lady from another table walked over to me. She said, "I'd like to help you on your journey back home." She handed me twenty dollars, and as I was leaving, other customers chipped in. I left there with nearly forty bucks.

I stepped outside as another customer was leaving. He asked me, "Are you heading north?"

I said, "Yes, Denver." I threw my suitcase in the back of his pickup and climbed in. He asked me about my faith, and I shared with him how I came to know Jesus. We traveled about fifty miles. Then he said, "This is where I turn off. I'm headed to Santa Fe."

We came to the exit and he pulled onto the shoulder. "Would you pray with me?" he asked.

I prayed for the Lord to reveal Himself to him in a way that left no room for doubt as to who He is and how He can change lives. I told him I was learning to put my faith in God and not in the words of men. As I got out, he handed me a fifty-dollar bill.

I walked ahead up the onramp back onto I-25. Another pickup truck pulled up alongside me and the driver reached across and opened the passenger door. "Sorry," he said, "the outside handle is broken. How far are you going?"

I told him Denver, and he said he could get me to Raton, New Mexico. I climbed in, and he told me his name was Juan. I introduced myself, and he said it was great that we shared the same name. We talked about faith also. He told me he had eleven teenaged boys and young men living on his ranch who had all been homeless at one time or another. Then he said, "I try to help them as best I can. Some are runaways, most are Native American, but they all need help."

I asked him, "How do you make ends meet with so many?"

He said, "God provides. I think He provided you this evening. Will you come join us for a big old pot of venison stew? We always have community dinner on Saturdays. You can also spend the night if you wish." I said I would. He added, "I was actually hoping you would tell them your story. Perhaps they might find what you have found."

I asked, "Do you guys go to a church nearby?"

"We did. But recently our pastor died so we've just been studying at home on Sunday mornings."

I was surprised that the kids bowed their heads and prayed before dinner was served. The stew was great and the conversation was just what I needed. Telling others what Jesus had done for me was a timely reminder for me, too.

Morning came and breakfast was big and filling. Lots of bacon and eggs with toast and pan-fried potatoes, orange juice, and coffee.

Juan drove me back to the interstate, and, as I was getting out of the truck, he offered me a twenty.

I said, "No, you keep it. I have money, and you have a lot of mouths to feed."

He said, "God told me to give it to you, so please let me."

I took the twenty and thanked him. Rides the rest of the way to Denver were both short and quick. I never sat too long waiting, and each ride also came with offers of cash to help me with my journey.

The last ride into Denver dropped me off at Broadway and Evans, just after 10:00 P.M. I was sitting at a bus stop waiting for a bus to take me to Jack and Fawnda's apartment on East Quincy in southeast Denver.

I sat there and looked for the bus to come down Broadway and turn left onto Evans and pick me up. Instead of a bus, a motorcycle came down Broadway. As it turned and passed by me, the girl's purse fell from the back, tumbled over towards me, and came to rest right below my feet. I looked down at it.

I felt like the Lord was saying to me, "Which John are you going to be?"

There was the John who would look through the purse and take the cash, then shove the rest down the gutter right next to me. There was the other John who would see that it got back to whoever it was who'd lost it. I opened my suitcase, shoved the purse inside, and latched the case back shut.

Just then a police officer came around the corner and pulled up to me. He rolled the passenger window down and asked, "What are you up to this evening?"

I said, "I'm just waiting for the bus."

He said, "The last bus by here was a half hour ago. Where you heading?"

"Whispering Pines West Apartments—7335 East Quincy Avenue."

He said, "You're kidding me. That's where I live! I'm on my way home now. Jump in I'll give you a lift."

The short twenty-minute trip was just enough to tell him about my coming back to the Lord. I left out all the details about my adventures with Walt.

As we pulled into the parking lot of the apartments, I thanked him for the ride. I asked if I could pray for him and he said yes. I prayed he would be safe, that he would grow closer to the Lord each day, and that he would trust Him for guidance.

He said afterward, "Thank you, John."

CHAPTER FORTY-ONE

TO DO IT RIGHT

Sunday Evening, August 26, 1984

I knocked on the apartment door and Fawnda answered. She said, "Oh, so it's you."

I asked, "What do you mean?"

She said, "God told us earlier to move Jessica into our room with us and prepare her room, because we would be having a guest coming to stay with us."

Jack wanted to know all about my past six months. I told him everything. He was talking to me like a father who had just picked his child up from the detention hall.

I opened my suitcase and handed the purse to Jack. "This fell off a motorcycle and rolled over to my feet," I said. "I didn't even look inside, so I have no idea who it belongs to."

Jack looked inside and exclaimed, "No problem, John! This girl goes to my church. I'll give it to her later this week." I took that as a sign from God that I was indeed doing the right thing, and that I was on the right path.

Fawnda was interested in how I was doing emotionally and spiritually. I told her I was feeling a lot of remorse for walking away from God and was glad to be back. Jack told me they were planning a work day at the church first thing in the morning. If I got up before seven I could have breakfast and then go help.

Monday, August 27, 1984

The next morning we had a big breakfast and then went to the church to work. There we found about a dozen volunteers from Jack's congregation. We worked all day and cleaned up the lawn, painted the outside of the building, and repaired several of the chairs and tables. Then we cleaned the kitchen and children's rooms.

When we were winding down for the day, I asked Jack if I could get a ride home with him so I could shower and do some laundry. "Fawnda and I have to stay and meet with a couple for coffee," he said, "so would you please catch a ride with her?" He gestured to a girl who had been helping us.

Fawnda asked Jack and me to come to the back room to talk. She said to Jack, "I really don't think that's a good idea." I also asked Jack to find another way.

He said, "Why are you freaking out, John? It's just a ride home."

I got in the pickup truck she was driving, and we headed toward the apartment. Then suddenly she turned and went the other way. I asked, "Why are we going this way?"

She said, "I need to stop by my house to change clothes first."

She ran in, and in a few minutes came back out wearing a skimpy tube top and shorts. I immediately felt defeated and powerless.

I first got angry with myself, then had to control myself because I didn't want to cry. I just wanted to get out of there fast. I was thinking, Nothing has changed with *me*. All I wanted was to find a wife, but it still seemed the Christian women I was meeting just threw themselves at any man who was single.

I was upset, and I didn't talk at all on the way home. By the time I walked in the door, Jack and Fawnda were already there. As soon as I saw Fawnda, I started to cry. I couldn't help it. The discouragement was more than I could take.

Jack walked in from the bedroom, saw me crying, and asked, "What happened to you?

❖ ❖ ❖

Tuesday, August 28, 1984

The next morning I didn't want to go to the church for another work day but Jack insisted.

He said, "You are going to have to face your fears. You can't run from everything. That's why you left Denver before the spring."

I wasn't afraid. I just didn't want to see that girl.

Fortunately she didn't show up for the work detail. We spent the day repairing the roof and resurfacing the stage. They had found a drummer while I was gone, so I set up the drums and wired the stage for microphone plugs and several 110 outlets. I helped move the pulpit back into position, and we locked up for the evening.

I was sad and didn't talk on the way home. Every time Fawnda tried to console me, Jack would start back in lecturing.

CHAPTER FORTY-TWO

MERCY AND GRACE

Wednesday, August 26, 1984

Jack, Fawnda, and I showed up at church about an hour early. I mistakenly assumed that I would be leading worship.

Jack said, "Of course not, John. You just came off of a six-month backslide and you think you are worthy to lead worship? Not to mention your little escapade Monday evening. It'll be a while before God restores you to that position."

Sitting on the front row was a lady named Vicki, whom I had met in Tulsa at Kenneth Hagin's church. She was in Jack's classes at Rhema and was visiting Denver. I stood in front of the pulpit talking to Jack as he introduced me to Michael Ball, who would be leading worship. I shook his hand and looked around to decide where to sit.

Vicki offered me the seat to her right, next to the center aisle, by the pulpit where Jack would be speaking. As the music started, a young lady came in and sat on the other side of Vicki. It was obvious they knew each other.

Once Jack started speaking I couldn't help but notice that the lady on the other side of Vicki kept leaning forward and looking at me. By the end of the message it had become a bit awkward. Then, as Jack said the closing prayer and dismissed us, she ran around Vicki to speak to me.

"So," she said, "Who are you, anyway?"

I said, "Excuse me?"

Just then I heard God say, "John, this is your wife."

We went to have coffee along with a few other young people from the church. We went to the Village Inn in Cinderella City, a shopping mall in Englewood just a couple of miles from the church. She introduced herself as Raylene.

"Are you from Texas?" she asked.

I said, "Well, yes. I am. Is that a problem?"

"No, should it be?" We talked through the evening and I told her about my journey back to Denver. She said that during that time she had been in prayer for two and a half days straight. I realized that the days paralleled the time I was stranded under the bridge.

"What kind of man are you looking for?" I asked.

She answered, "I'm not looking for a man."

I told her, "God said you are my wife."

She said, "I know. As I walked into the church I saw the back of your head, and God told me that you are my husband."

I said, "I thought you weren't looking for a man."

"I'm not," she answered.

One of the guys with us was named Ken Wallace. Ken said to me, "Jack asked me to tag along and give you a ride to his house when we are done here."

Raylene and I said our goodbyes, and Ken drove me hone. Turns out, Jack had sent Wallace to keep an eye on us. A chaperone, to make sure we didn't fall into sin.

The next day Jack took me to the house of an older lady named Lois. She needed some wallpaper hung—something I was good at. She said it wasn't wise to drive to her place every day from Jack's house and then have to drive back in the evening. "So, John, why not just move your things into the front bedroom and stay here? I have plenty of work to keep you busy for a few weeks."

I did. She also asked that I drive her 1973 Dodge Swinger, so it didn't get all seized up from just sitting there. She hadn't driven it in a couple of years.

Raylene and I would meet every day for coffee at noon when she was on lunch break. I would bring her flowers and small plaques I had purchased at the Christian bookstore in the mall. I told her everything about my past, including my time in prison and what for. I told her I had been a bouncer, a biker, a musician . . . and a stripper. I wanted nothing hidden from her. I needed her to know everything about who I was.

Jack threw a party at the house of one of the couples who attended the church. Everyone was invited. Jack began baptizing people in the pool. Raylene was there along with her grandmother, Ida, or Granny as she was called. I spent the day following Raylene through the rooms and around the pool. I would anticipate which room she was headed to and strategically position myself there. Then I would ask her if she was following me. We both knew, however, it was actually me following her.

During our coffee time the next day, Raylene said, "My mother is perhaps the closest person to God I have ever known. She hears God clearly and always obeys Him."

Then she told me, "Granny went home from the party and talked to my mom. She said, 'I think Raylene has met the man she is supposed to marry.'

"Mom wanted me to tell her about you, so I said, 'He's a musician.'

" 'And?' Mom asked.'

" 'And he is a biker,' I told her.

" 'And?' she asked again.

" 'And he used to rob banks.'

"Then Mom told me, 'You know, in the natural, it doesn't sound too good. But once you get into the Spirit, it's definitely a God thing.' "

That evening I prayed and told God I didn't want to date Raylene until I could treat her with the respect she deserved. I wanted to make sure we honored our commitment to doing it right.

At lunch the next day, I met with Raylene again. I told her, "We can't go out on a date. I want to make sure I don't mess this thing up."

She said, "I prayed last night that you wouldn't take me out until you could treat me like a godly woman should be treated."

The next afternoon, we told Jack we were going to get married.

I said, "God told both Raylene and I that we are to get married."

Jack answered, "I don't believe it is of God."

I said, "Jack, you always said the best time to obey God is right now."

He answered, "You are making another mistake, John. I think you are letting your need for affection get the best of you. You are thinking with the wrong body parts."

"God said get married so we are going to," I told him.

"If you insist, then we will start counseling. You need six months just to get to where you should be spiritually. Then we will start pre-marital counseling for the two of you. If you both still want to get married, then we will see."

"No," I said. "We want to get married right away."

Jack came back with, "Unless you submit to counseling first, I won't do the marriage."

I said, "We will find someone else to marry us."

He then said, "In that case, you are not welcome in my church."

I said, "If you insist."

"I do," he replied. "And I want you to know that you will not be able to lead worship anywhere. No one will have you because you are following your flesh and not the Spirit."

Raylene and I left the church. She took me home and introduced me to her mother, Maxine.

Maxine said, "You two should check out a church in Aurora called International Gospel Fellowship."

I said, "Sounds good to me."

CHAPTER FORTY-THREE

YELLOW ROSES

The next Sunday we were at International Gospel Fellowship when the doors opened. To be honest, I felt like we had found a home the minute we walked in. Immediately after the worship, the pastor walked up and introduced himself to us.

He said, "Hi, my name is John Webb. This your first time here?"

I said, "Yes, it is."

He said, "You're a musician, aren't you?"

I nodded and he added, "Stick around after the service. We should talk."

I had no idea what he would want to talk to me about, but Raylene and I decided to stay. When the service was over, he came back to us and asked, "Guitar?"

"Yes," I said, "and harmonica."

He said, "God told me that you are to play in the band, so you should bring your guitar next Sunday and audition." He started to walk away. Then he stopped and turned back. "Forget the audition," he said. "If God said you should be in the band, you don't need to audition. Just come ready to play."

We spent the week making wedding plans. I wanted to just go get married right away, but Raylene said we needed to do invites and actually plan things out. It was all starting to come together.

Then we were at coffee again. I handed her the bouquet of red roses as I always did. "I am just about set with this whole thing," she said, "but I want to make sure I'm not making a mistake again."

"I can understand that," I said. "Sounds reasonable."

She added, "So I have asked for God to send me one more sign that I am supposed to marry you."

That took me by surprise and really annoyed me. But I was careful not to let her see I was exploding inside. I said, "I'm sure everything will be okay."

As she left, I started a heated conversation with God. "What is the problem with this woman You sent me? You told her. You told me. That's it. Now she wants another sign? That's crazy, God. You know I miss it and sometimes I don't hear You as well as I need to. I probably won't get the sign, and the wedding will be off, all because I missed it."

God said, "Just meet her tomorrow for lunch, and we'll talk some sense into her head."

The next day I arrived at the mall with plenty of time to pick up some flowers for Raylene. I walked into the cooler at the florist, and grabbed the typical red roses. Then I thought, *I always get red roses, I should get something different.* I looked around and saw pink roses. *No,* I thought, *that's no good.* Then I saw yellow roses and thought, *No, yellow means friendship. That's not what we are going for here.* I decided to go back to the red roses, but as I picked them up I could see they looked old and wilted. I realized I was running out of time so I just grabbed the yellow ones and paid.

I ran down the mall to the Village Inn and took my seat in a booth. I laid the flowers next to me on the seat. I was hoping she wouldn't be disappointed by not getting red ones.

Raylene walked in and took the other side of the booth.

God said, "Just hand her the flowers, then we will straighten her out."

As I handed the yellow roses to her, she looked shocked. *She's disappointed,* I thought.

She said, "Oh Lord."

I asked, "Are you okay?"

She said, "I said to God, 'If I am to marry John, have him bring me yellow roses."

I was almost in tears. Then I heard God say, "Right. Talk some sense into her. Straighten her out, Mr. 'I Can't Hear God'."

❖ ❖ ❖

The following Sunday, we got to church early so Pastor Webb could introduce me to the band and we could run through a few songs. I played guitar on everything and sang. I also added harmonica on a couple of songs. The congregation liked it.

After the service, Pastor Webb said, "John, I want you to take over as worship leader. I believe God sent you because I have been really over-stretched trying to lead worship and preach also."

I said, "I think I should just be part of the band for at least a few weeks to start. I don't want others thinking this outsider just moved in and took over."

The pastor wasn't really pleased, but he went along anyway.

The following Sunday, he asked me to help pick out the songs for the service. He also asked that I take the lead vocals on a couple. By the time the service started, I was pretty much placed in charge. No one was put out by me leading, so I guess I became the worship leader even though I'd wanted to wait.

CHAPTER FORTY-FOUR

MY GIFT FROM GOD

Wednesday, October 17, 1984

I was driving over to see Raylene after she got home from work, praying and asking God what I could do to help make this a better marriage. I wanted to make sure we would be able to build it with as little stress as possible.

God said to me, "When you get there, take out your checkbook and ask Raylene to bring out all her bills."

I did, and then God told me to pay them all off. I had no debt and was making pretty good money working for Lois. The bills almost drained the bank account, but I was confident God would take care of us.

Between Raylene and her mother, Maxine, the wedding began to take shape. They arranged for a small church to hold the ceremony and a friend donated their house for the reception.

Raylene wanted a unique ring, so she wanted to buy a diamond and design a ring for it. She told me she'd heard God say He wanted her to spend only five hundred dollars on a ring.

Our mutual friend, Vicki, knew a girl in Tulsa who had been engaged but the guy had broken it off. The girl said she would sell us the diamond from her ring for five hundred. But when she sent the diamond, it was still in her ring. She said we could have the rings to melt down and create our own. However the rings she sent were unique, and both Raylene and I loved them. Lois, the older lady I was living with, gave us the five hundred, saying God had told her to give us exactly that amount to buy a ring.

Someone bought me a gold band and we were set.

Maxine asked Jerry Brandt, a minister friend of the family, to do the service and he accepted. In addition, two musicians and singers donated their services. My mother and younger brother, David, flew into town. David was my best man.

Friday, October 19, 1984

Jerry did an amazing service. He read: "For I know the plans I have for you," declares the Lord, "plans to prosper you and not to harm you, plans to give you hope and a future. Then you will call on me and come and pray to me, and I will listen to you. You will seek me and find me when you seek me with all your heart" (Jeremiah 29:11-13).

It wasn't exactly the same verse, but it reminded me once again of the scripture on the card that Pastor Mark Miller gave me before I left Denver: "Then you will call, and the Lord will answer; you will cry for help, and he will say: Here am I" (Isaiah 58:9).

The message was followed by prophecy. The minister of the small church had recorded a cassette of songs he thought we would like and then made an audio tape of the ceremony for us. We had a photographer, and a videographer. All in all, it was pretty awesome.

For the honeymoon, we went to the Park Suite Hotel in downtown Denver for two nights. By Sunday morning, we were back in church.

In addition to leading worship at the church, we also began helping with children's church. Raylene started assisting with the church office duties and running the church's food and clothing bank, called Christian Loving Care. I had begun teaching a men's Bible breakfast, and Raylene and I started holding a home fellowship meeting in our home every Tuesday evening. All that, along with Tuesday night worship team practice, made our schedule tight.

The pastor had initiated several home fellowship groups but they all seemed to fizzle out within a few weeks. Except ours. It grew to about twenty to twenty-five people.

I knew the formula for leading worship in a charismatic church. Three fast songs, two slow songs, followed by some Uoo-la-las. Then we laid hands on somebody. But I really liked the slow songs. I wasn't interested in getting everyone all wound up. All I wanted was to close my eyes and worship God. Then I would open my eyes to see if anyone went with me. They always did. However, Pastor Webb began to get annoyed with my worship leading. Quite often he would say things like, "John, you need to keep your eyes open when you lead worship." Or, "When are you going to do some fast songs?"

Finally one day he said to me, "John, by next Sunday you need to be prepared to do a couple of fast songs."

That week I practiced and came up with two fast songs I felt comfortable doing: "I Will Magnify The Lord" and "Open the Eyes of My Heart, Lord."

That Sunday I did them both.

But I did them real slow.

CHAPTER FORTY-FIVE

CROSS & CLEF MINISTRIES

In 1985, ten years after being released from prison, while we were still attending International Gospel Fellowship, Raylene and I started an evangelistic ministry called Cross & Clef Ministries. By this time, I had written several country gospel and folk gospel songs and was leading people to know Jesus personally as often as I could. I told everyone who would listen (and even some who wouldn't) what God had done for me, and how He saved me and delivered me from drug addiction and alcoholism. I preached, sang in churches, and shared my testimony. I encouraged people to forgive the people who had treated them badly, so God could forgive them.

I found a job as a process server, which had me spending every day, all day, driving around Colorado handing out summonses, subpoenas, and restraining orders. I would put a cassette from the Bible in the car stereo and listen to the Word of God the entire day. Each day was a different book of the Bible. Every two months, I would finish the entire Bible and start over with Genesis again. My days were spent listening and talking to God.

Then, in the spring of 1987, our son Bo was born and my life changed. Shortly after his birth, I was driving along in a deep conversation with God.

"God, I don't understand it," I said. "How could You send Your Son to die for me? I'm just a sinner. Actually, I'm one of the worst. Yet I would gladly throw myself in front of a car to save my son's life. There is no way I could ever let my son die for me or for anyone. I love him too much."

God said to me, "Hypothetical situation. Let's say you have twelve kids. If I asked you to give me one of them, which one would you give up?"

Without hesitation I said, "A strong one, the most independent one."

God asked, "Why that one?"

I answered, "Because he could handle it and eventually he would understand."

God said, "You sound just like your mother."

I pulled the car to the curb and cried. In that moment, I realized that Barbara Bliss, the prison psychiatrist, had been wrong when she said my healing would come by accepting the fact that my mother didn't love me. I also realized how wrong the Christians were who said my healing would come by forgiving my mother for not loving me.

The truth is, my healing was in finding how wrong I was in my believing that my mother *didn't* love me. For the first time in my life, I understood how much Mom loved me. I sat there on the side of the road for well over an hour before I could get it together enough to continue on.

I started feeling like God wanted us to leave International Gospel Fellowship Church but I didn't know where He wanted us to go. *That can't be God*, I thought. *Look at everything we are involved in. We have invested so much in our ministry at IGF.* I didn't want to disobey God, but I wanted to make sure it really was Him telling me we should leave.

One day in prayer, I heard God say, "Leave that church, or I will shut your ministries down." The next morning Raylene went to the building where the church food and clothing bank was housed. She found an eviction notice on the door.

Tuesday evening, our home fellowship group was packed. Even people who had attended and moved away were there visiting from out of town. I felt like God wanted us to tell them goodbye. We spent that evening discussing God's plan for our lives and letting everyone know we would be leaving. The next morning, I showed up for my men's breakfast; I ate alone. Pastor Webb's wife, Sharon, called to tell Raylene she was taking over the church office duties. Then, finally, I showed up for church Sunday morning and Pastor Webb was there with his guitar. He said, "Don't worry, John. I just miss sitting in. You are in charge. I'm just going to play along if you don't mind."

"Sure," I said. "No problem."

Then he stepped up to the microphone and said, "Good morning, everyone. For our first song this morning, we will be doing, 'This is the Day.'" He took over, and it was like I could hear God repeating His words to me: *I will shut down your ministries.*

Right after the service I told the pastor we were leaving the church.

CHAPTER FORTY-SIX

ROGER

My songwriting really took off after that, and by 1990 I was singing at churches almost every Sunday. Occasionally I was asked to speak to groups of new believers and to share my testimony in coffee houses where Bible studies were being held.

During this time, God gave me a vision for feeding the homeless. In the vision, I was standing in the back of a pickup truck parked under a viaduct, handing out sack lunches and cartons of milk. I told everyone I knew about it, and they all said it sounded like a God thing. But they also said, "In God's perfect timing."

I was frustrated with everyone agreeing with me but telling me to hold off, and I began to be really annoyed with the wait-on-God theology. Finally, I sat down and prayed to ask God why I had to wait. First, He reminded me of George Todd and his observation about building a yacht: more time planning and less time building. Then God reminded me of George's final comment: "Of course, if you want it to float, it's gonna take a bit longer."

God said to me, "I want you to make all the mistakes on paper before you start. These are real people, not boats, and you can't be changing things as you go. Run everything through your head and on paper until all the bugs are worked out. Then we will begin."

During this time, I was working at Cherry Hills Community Church as head of maintenance. I considered myself a minister but was still waiting for God to open the doors for full-time ministry.

"How can you call yourself a minister when you still smoke?" people would wonder. It bothered me also. I had actually tried to quit smoking dozens of times. By the way, quitting smoking is expensive. You throw away your pack of cigarettes, then go buy another. You throw out the ashtrays, then go buy new ones.

Still, friends would say to me, "Can you justify smoking from the Bible?"

I responded, "It says smoking is okay right next to where it says it's okay to judge people." It was a never-ending frustration to me. I prayed. I prayed often. Nothing.

Then one evening I said to God, "God, why did You instantly take away alcoholism and drug addiction from me, but You left cigarettes?"

He said, "I took them away, and I will take away cigarettes. It's My timing, not yours."

I asked, "God, why can't I just stop?"

God answered, "Because you are trying to please men and not Me."

That day I decided not to worry again about smoking. I quit trying to quit. When people asked about my smoking, I told them it was between me and God, not me and them.

I was fairly successful in not worrying about it for while, until Raylene and I were invited to Estes Park, Colorado, for the Christian Artists of the Rockies event. I showcased my songs for some of the national artists and participated in a few workshops. As Raylene and I were driving back home, God spoke to me. "Quit smoking tomorrow," He said.

I said, "Raylene, God said I am to quit smoking tomorrow."

"Okay," she said, "we'll throw out the ashtrays and spray air freshener in the house to get the smell out."

I said, "No, I don't think that is necessary. I think this time is different."

The next morning, I woke up and went to work as usual. At noon, I went out to a picnic table to have my lunch. While I was sitting there, Tom, one of the maintenance workers, joined me. He shook out a cigarette and then offered me one. I hadn't even noticed that I'd gone all morning without smoking or even desiring to. It hadn't occurred to me.

"No, thank you," I said. "I quit."

I have not smoked since.

Early in 1993, Jerry Brandt, the minister who married Raylene and me, called and asked if I would go to Seattle with him to help with an event for the homeless and play at a few churches, I accepted. We arrived and began setting up in the park at Pioneer Square in downtown Seattle. The four days were packed full of ministry and prayer times. It couldn't have been more different than how I used to spend my time in Seattle.

As we were onstage the last day, a man came up and introduced himself as Roger Jensen. "Do you have any recordings of your songs?" he asked.

I told him, "Actually, no."

He said, "God just told me and my wife that we are to help you record a cassette of your original stuff in our recording studio. Do you have enough songs for a full cassette?"

I said, "Well, yes, in fact I do." Then I asked him, "Did God happen to say how much you are going to charge me for the sessions?"

Roger answered, "He told us to provide the studio, supplies, musicians, and our spare bedroom to help you complete the project. No charge." We spent the evening discussing a plan, and I left feeling pretty good about my new project.

The next afternoon after church, Jerry asked me to join him as he met for lunch with the elders of the organization that held his ordination—the Ministerial Fellowship and International Church. "It's a long name," Jerry explained, "but they are legit. Years ago they were called the John G. Lake Society."

At lunch, conversation quickly turned to me. The elders had plenty of questions about what I believed and what my stands were on several controversial issues. I asked, "Why all the questions?"

The most senior of them answered, "Jerry has requested that we ordain you, and it is standard protocol."

After several hours of interrogation, they began the process of ordination. They laid hands on me and prayed for me. Each person present then spoke life over my ministry (words of encouragement and prophetic insight) and asked God to show me clarity in my calling.

I flew back to Denver and shared with Raylene everything that happened. Three weeks later, I received my ordination certificate.

During the summer and fall of 1993, I took four trips to Seattle to work with Roger and his wife, Diane, on recording my album, *Crucified*. For the last trip, I brought my family with me. I had been bragging to them for years about how beautiful Seattle was and finally they got to see it as I did. They all fell in love with the entire state.

We flew home with two huge reels of one-inch tape containing the final mix of all the songs. On the plane back to Denver, Raylene and I talked. "Here is the plan," I said. "We will get one thousand dollars, and I've found a company that will produce cassettes for me at one dollar each."

Raylene answered, "Kristina said she wants to help with the one thousand."

I said, "We can sell cassettes for ten dollars each. As soon as we sell two hundred cassettes, we'll take the two thousand dollars and go get CDs made. I can get them for two dollars each."

Raylene encouraged me wholeheartedly. "Sounds like a plan," she said firmly.

We had friends lined up to help with the graphics and with printing the liner notes. We did a photo shoot for the cover, and Raylene got some amazing shots. Production took about a month, from converting the reels to digital audio recordings to all the design and printing, duplicating the cassettes, stuffing the liner notes, and shrink-wrapping the final product. Finally, they were delivered.

The next Sunday, I was asked to sing a couple of songs at Colorado Community Church. I helped Raylene set up a cassette table in the lobby before the service and then got ready to sing. I sang "The Toll" and "The Fisherman," both songs from my album. As soon as the service was over, I joined Raylene at the table to help her with sales. After we finished, we quickly packed up and headed to the house. I counted up the cash and found we had sold exactly two hundred cassettes. Two thousand dollars!

As I walked into the bedroom, I thought, *God is blessing my plan.* I tossed the money onto the bed and shouted, "Yes! Time to get the CDs made."

Just then I heard God say, "No. Time to feed the homeless."

I said, "But God, they said You have perfect timing."

CHAPTER FORTY-SEVEN

MORNING MANNA

We went out that evening and bought enough supplies to make one hundred sack lunches, which we put together each night. We wrote out scriptures and made sure there was one in each lunch.

The next morning I drove downtown and prayed along the way. "God, I don't know what I am doing. I've never done this before. I have no idea where to go. So You are going to have to show me."

I came to the corner of 21st and Broadway, where I saw a sign that read, "Coalition for the Homeless." I figured I must be where I belonged. I got out and handed a sack lunch to the first person who walked by. Within just a few minutes, I was out of lunches.

While handing out the lunches, I had a vision of a place where the homeless could come in out of the weather and get free coffee. A place where they could get a hot meal and change their clothes. A place with lockers, where they could take a shower and do a load of laundry. A place where they could hang out and feel safe. Where they could receive mail and possibly find a job or even a roommate.

I told the homeless men, women, and children, "Come back tomorrow. I'll be back with more."

Each evening, we put together lunches. I managed to get one of the local dairies to deliver cartons of milk to our house. Someone donated a used commercial fridge, and we set it up in our garage.

I started writing a monthly newsletter telling everyone I knew about our food line and asking if they wanted to help. Soon, people were coming to help hand out lunches, and we added a large coffee pot. We had volunteers for every day and donations started coming in to help buy the food. We started feeding a hundred people each day except Sundays, when I would be speaking or singing at churches around the state to help raise money for supplies.

A few months later, God told me to go talk to the Catholic diocese at Logan and Colfax. They had been handing out sandwiches through a small opening in their back door, and there were a few homeless people hanging around. I asked for a meeting with the monsignor and he agreed to see me.

I brought with me one of the sandwiches they had given away. It was a stale salami sandwich on moldy bread with mustard. It stunk. I also brought in one of our sack lunches, which included two bologna and cheese sandwiches on fresh bread, two cookies, an orange, a scripture, a multi-vitamin, a cup of coffee, and a carton of milk.

I told him, "You guys are serving about thirty people a day. If we work together, we can serve more people and do a better job of it."

The monsignor asked, "What caused you to want to take care of the less fortunate?"

I answered, "I remember as a child the times when my mom would take us behind the Safeway stores in Dallas, and my younger brother and I would get the discarded food from the dumpsters. I remember my mom, with a razor blade, cutting the bad parts off of peaches and handing the good parts to the five of us to eat. I never really saw that necessarily being a bad time in my life. Things like that, while embarrassing to older siblings, can be adventurous to an eight- and six-year-old.

"I remember the time I lived in a shelter in Montana and the time spent living on the streets of Las Vegas and the times I slept under a bridge in Albuquerque. I think of the times I woke up in strange places without a clue where I was or how I got there. I think of how I have wasted my life either drunk, high, or both, yet I'm still alive today in spite of myself. I suppose you could pick a reason from this list—any of them would be a fitting answer. But the truth is, these things really didn't compel me to choose my ministry. God did."

By the next day, Morning Manna had a home, and within two years we were up to two hundred and fifty lunches a day. We were also giving away about five hundred pairs of socks each month.

❖ ❖ ❖

One day, I saw a sign in a restroom that read,

Let your light shine into darkness,
*so the others **too** might find the way out.*

I noticed that the word *too* was bold and underlined. I said to God, "That's what I want, to let my light shine. Show me how."

That night I dreamed I was in total darkness, and I couldn't see anything. It was as if I were blind. Suddenly, a flashlight appeared high above me. It was waving around as if searching for something. Then it stopped and shone squarely on my face. Immediately, I saw a hand reach out past the light towards me. I took the hand, and, as it began lifting me up, I could see it was God. He handed me the flashlight and said, "Shine it back into the darkness."

A few days later, I was reading the Bible. I was in Isaiah. When I got to chapter 58, I again remembered the card Pastor Mark had given me: "Then you will call, and the LORD will answer; you will cry for help, and he will say: Here am I" (Isaiah 58:9). From there I read the rest of verse 9 and verse 10: "If you do away with the yoke of oppression, with the pointing finger and malicious talk, and if you spend yourselves in behalf of the hungry and satisfy the needs of the oppressed, then your light will rise in the darkness, and your night will become like the noonday" (Isaiah 58:9-10).

I froze. It was talking about letting my light shine. I backed up and reread the passage. This time the portion, "Spend yourselves in behalf of the hungry," popped out at me. God said, "That doesn't mean give to the poor. It doesn't mean volunteer. It says, 'Spend yourself.'"

I knew that I had found my life verse. As long as I am an air pump, I'm not "spent" yet. If I look down and my chest is still rising and falling, I am still under the call.

We started holding a July 4th barbeque each year where we served hamburgers and hotdogs to about five hundred people, along with chips, potato salad, coleslaw, and cans of pop. And every year on Thanksgiving and Christmas mornings, we would hold a big breakfast for about five hundred homeless. We served bacon, sausage, eggs, pan fries, toast, orange juice, and coffee. We also had muffins and cinnamon rolls. We gave out sleeping bags, hats, coats, gloves, socks, and backpacks. There were a few times at Christmas and Thanksgiving when we had almost as many volunteers as we did homeless.

We also started putting together what we called Care Kits. We took one-gallon Ziploc bags and put in a pair of socks and a toothbrush. We added travel-sized toothpaste, a bar of soap, a pack of gum, and hand warmers, along with a few Band-Aids and a power bar. We found volunteers to assemble the Care Kits and soon we were distributing about two hundred kits each month.

Sometimes homeless mothers or couples would approach us and ask us to take their babies into our home. They preferred trusting us with their children over getting them caught up in the social services system.

Zaier was a small baby with spina bifida and clubbed feet. His mother left him with us and headed to Indiana. A couple of months later, she returned and retrieved him. J. J. was five years old. His mother and father left him with us for a few months. Our son Bo prayed with him to receive salvation a few weeks before his mother asked us to return him. Then there was Beca, a six-month-old baby girl who stayed with us for nearly a year. We were always heartbroken when our time with each of these kids came to an end.

CHAPTER FORTY-EIGHT

THE TOLLGATE

One of the songs God gave me is called "The Toll." It's a metaphor for the fact that no matter how much money you have or how much you have done, it's not enough to get you into Heaven.

I had a friend named John Robinson who, like me, was a street minister. He also had a church on East Colfax Street near downtown Denver. Often, he would help us hand out food. Sometimes he would go out and serve the homeless with us, handing out socks and bottles of water in the alleys.

One morning, Robinson came to the food line and asked if I would join him for a cup of coffee after we finished in the alley. At coffee, I asked, "What's up, Praise Jesus?" That's what everyone called him because he always wore a t-shirt that had "Praise Jesus" printed on the front.

"Are you still wanting to do a coffee house?" he asked.

"More than ever," I answered.

"I'm getting ready to move back to New York and wanted to know if you would be interested in taking over the building I'm leasing," he said.

"Well, that depends. How much is the lease?"

"We're paying two thousand a month, but I think the landlord will be willing to go down a bit."

We went to the building, and I could see it needed a ton of work and cleaning before we would be able to do anything in it.

Later that day, I met with the board of our ministry, and they were all in favor of seeing if we could make a go of it. Praise Jesus took me to meet with the landlord, Mr. Vagnino. We came to an agreement of a new two-year lease at fifteen hundred a month. He also gave us the first two months free in order to get the place cleaned out and try to get most of the repair work done.

We named it The Tollgate Coffeehouse after my song, "The Toll." We began remodeling, painting, and decorating. I had already been collecting street signs and license plates we could use in the decor. I had joined a license plate collectors club called ALPCA. Through it, I traded plates with people all over the world. By the time we had The Tollgate open, I had well over three thousand plates on the walls. We had every year of Colorado plates dating back as far as the state first issued them: 1913. We also had, from each of the fifty states, a plate from my birth year, 1952— including Hawaii and Alaska, even though they weren't yet states.

I also had a 1952 license plate from each of the Canadian provinces, as well about twenty-five other 1952s from around the world. We displayed an old gas pump and a fire hydrant, and above each bathroom door we hung service-station gas-price signs. We had also collected street lights to hang from the ceiling, real working green, yellow, and red lights. And we had flashing yellow caution lights.

We provided a shower for the homeless and installed two washers and two dryers so we could do a load of laundry for anyone who came in. We opened every day right after we finished the food line.

We served coffee and tea along with pastries, and at lunch we served a hot meal. We installed lockers so the homeless could stash their belongings, and we started letting them use The Tollgate as their mailing address. It was a safe, warm place to get out of the weather and hang out between day-labor jobs. We played cards and dominoes. We had a movie every Thursday.

We were open Monday through Saturday, and on Sundays I was preaching or singing around Denver to raise funds for the coffeehouse. I was praying and thanking God for finally opening The Tollgate, and I told him I wanted a church to partner with so the homeless could have a place to worship and The Tollgate wouldn't go dead on Sundays.

The Toll

VERSE 1
Walking down life's long lonesome highway,
No one there to help carry my load.
I'm so tired of trying to do it my way,

Somehow it seems I'm not even on the right road.

CHORUS 1
Save me, come on save me.
I'm so tired and, Lord, I'm so cold.
Save me, someone save me.
Pick me up, I'm down, please save my soul.

VERSE 2
There's a tollgate up ahead on the highway,
Not a penny in my pocket can I show.
As the tears fall down my face and hit the roadway,
I cry, Someone help me please, and pay my toll.

CHORUS 2
Save me, someone save me.
Turn my life around, save my soul
Save me, come on save me.
Someone save my life, pay my toll.

VERSE 3
As the car pulled up and the big door swung wide open,
He said, "Hop in, son, seems you could use a ride."
Then He dropped the coin down into the tollgate,
He said, "Rest your head now, son, you're safe inside."

CHORUS 3
Saved me, My Lord, saved me.
From out of the darkness and the cold.
Safely, now I'm safely,
Safely with my Lord on my way home.

CHORUS 4
Take me, come on, take me,
Take my heart, and take my soul.
Take me, come on take me,
Take me to the end of the road.
John Swanger, © 1987

The partner church didn't materialize right away but other assistance came along. A girl named Grace started helping us with Morning Manna, the food line. She was dating the drummer from a band called Five Iron Frenzy, a local but internationally famous Christian ska punk band. She started bringing band members down to help hand out the food. Soon, I became friends with most of the band. They actually did a couple of benefit concerts for our ministry and raised a couple of thousand dollars for food. I learned that the band, along with Pastor Mike Sares, had started a church called Scum of the Earth Church.

The name of the church came from 1 Corinthians 4:11-13:"To this very hour we go hungry and thirsty, we are in rags, we are brutally treated, we are homeless. We work hard with our own hands. When we are cursed, we bless; when we are persecuted, we endure it; when we are slandered, we answer kindly. Up to this moment we have become the scum of the earth, the refuse of the world." The church was formed for people who were either not welcomed or not ministered to in traditional churches. The tattooed, pierced, rainbow-haired, shatters, and punks. The disenfranchised and the broken. They called themselves "the church for the left-out and the right-brained."

Word got around that we had this large building and nothing going on, on Sundays. People started suggesting to us that Scum of the Earth was looking for a place to meet. I was too inwardly focused even to consider the thought of Scum being in our building. After all, the neighborhood already hated us for being there. They saw us as a place that brought the homeless into their community. The truth was, the homeless were already there; we were just giving them a place where they could get out of the weather and get out of the sight of the neighbors. So the thought of having a sign out front that said "Scum of the Earth" was a no-brainer as far as I was concerned.

Truthfully, after my prayer asking God to send a church to fill our space on Sundays, I had about seven different people suggest Scum. Every time, my response was swift and firm: "Not my problem." I was beginning to get frustrated, to the point that I was getting annoyed with people even suggesting the idea.

Then one morning I was sitting waiting for a service to start at New Community Christian Church, where Raylene and I had been attending.

A friend, Robbie Marshall, stopped by and tapped me on the shoulder. "Hey John," he said, "I'm going to go to Scum of the Earth this evening. Do you think you and Raylene might want to join me?"

I said, "I'll ask Raylene as soon as she parks and sits down. I'll let you know."

Then he added, "You know they are looking for a place to meet. They have already outgrown where they are."

I didn't answer, just gave him The Look.

Raylene sat down just a minute later, and I leaned over and whispered in her ear, "Robbie is going to Scum of the Earth this evening and has asked if we would like to join him."

She said, "I think that would be a great idea. By the way, did you know they are looking for a place to meet?"

I said, "That's not my concern."

Then the argument started. Not with Raylene, but with God. I explained to Him how it was a bad idea and how the troubles with the neighborhood would at least double. Finally, I told Him that I couldn't risk the ministry I had worked so long to build just so some punk rock group could have a place to hold their concerts.

God said to me, "*Your* ministry? If you insist, I'll get out of your way so I don't interfere."

I immediately repented. "God, You know that I never want to disobey You. I just always want to make sure it's You and not the enemy telling me to do something when it doesn't make sense to me."

God said, "I know. And I also know exactly how many times I have to tell you something before you finally get it."

I can't tell you what the sermon was that morning. I was busy downloading from God and trying to figure out how to move Scum of the Earth Church into The Tollgate Coffeehouse.

That evening we showed up at Scum. They were meeting in a small, old house on Marion Street. We were early, but one of the three girls setting up said we could come in and introduced herself to us. "Hi, my name is Deva. If you don't mind the noise, I was about to run through a few songs for this evening's service."

"Not at all," I told her.

The other two girls finished setting up a few chairs and sweeping. Then they threw a few pillows and cushions around on the floor. We sat and listened. I was surprised it wasn't loud, and it wasn't at all a rock concert. I thought, *This sounds just like regular church music, except it's good. Really good.*

The pastor, Mike, arrived and people just kept coming in. Soon the house was overcrowded and people began sitting on the front porch and back patio. They opened all the windows so everyone outside could hear. As the service started, Mike said a prayer, then they served dinner to everyone there.

"We're just visiting" I said.

A young girl named Hannah said, "That's okay, we feed everybody."

As the service ended, I went up to the pastor and asked, "Would you have time to go get a cup of coffee with us?"

He said, "I would, but I usually hang out with all the churchgoers. I need to spend time with them. Perhaps tomorrow?"

The next day we got together and I told Mike that God had told me that Scum was to move into The Tollgate Coffeehouse. I was shocked that he didn't jump at the chance. After all, wasn't it a God thing? Mike said, "I will take it to the leadership of our church, and we will pray about it."

A couple of weeks later, Mike called and asked if he could bring the church council to see The Tollgate. They showed up, and I gave them a tour of the building. We ended up in the basement, where they sat on the floor in a circle. They had a bunch of questions, but mostly they were just in awe of how cool the place looked and how big it was.

Chris Baker, one of the staff, asked, "How did you and Raylene meet?"

I shared how we met and how Raylene's first words to me were, "So, who are you, anyway?"

Chris rolled over to Deva, propped his head up on his hands in front of her, and asked, "So, who are you, anyway?" Everyone laughed.

Within a month, the church was moving in. I asked them what took so long. Deva said, "We wanted to make sure we could come without placing a negative impact on the neighborhood."

They rented the parking lot of an elementary school and printed some flyers to hand out to people coming to church:

Our new church facility is in The Tollgate Building
at the corner of Colfax and Ash.
Park at the school, don't park on Ash.
As you walk to church, you can pick up trash.
Take a trash bag home with you each week from Scum.

Within just a few weeks, it became obvious to Raylene and me that we had found our church home.

CHAPTER FORTY-NINE

LICENSE PLATES

The Automobile License Plate Collectors Association (ALPCA) I had joined held annual conventions at different cities around the country. In 2001, it was heading to Denver with more than five hundred collectors from all over the world bringing thousands of plates to display and trade. Among them, there were several collectors I had bought from and traded with, whom I knew only through making deals over the internet.

One of the people I dealt with used the name Bear as his online nickname. He called me and asked if I could line up a place where forty of us could meet for dinner. I booked us in a large restaurant with a private room that would accommodate us.

When we arrived, we took our seats around a large, long table. Bear was at the end, and I sat just to his right. He stood up and got everyone's attention. "We are going to introduce ourselves. Please stand and say your name, your online name, and where you are from." He gave his name, and added "Bear." Then told us he was from Miami, Florida.

He pointed to his left and said, "Let's start here and go around the table."

As he sat down, he said to me, "Aren't you Rev. John?"

I answered, "Yes."

He asked, "Could you please bless the food as you finish introducing yourself?"

One by one, the collectors all followed Bear's suit. It was nice to put a face to so many I had dealt with over the previous couple of years.

Finally, the guy just to my right stood up. "Hi," he said, "my name is Fred Agree, commonly known as The Geezer in the Freezer, and I'm from Trapper Creek, Alaska."

I was pleased to finally meet Fred, a man I'd done quite a bit of trading with. He was Jewish and always gave me a hard time, jokingly, about being Christian. He would tell me to throw away the fiction book and read the facts. He would slip a Kippah (or yarmulke) in with the license plates he would send me. I would often include either a New Testament or a crucifix in packages I sent to him. A couple of times, when his package arrived, I would find he had listed the return address as Buxom Bertha's XXX-Rated Videos. Fortunately, I had a wife whose humor was as tolerant as mine.

I stood and introduced myself. "Hi, I'm John Swanger, or Rev. John, and I am from right here in Denver. Bear has asked that I bless the food before we start."

As soon as I closed the prayer, Fred spoke. "Well," he said. "Now that they all know you are a preacher, why don't you tell them about robbing banks?" I'm sure everyone thought it would be great table conversation, but I was thinking, *testimony time.*

I had shared my testimony hundreds of times and always talked about prison. Usually, I included Paul Stavenjord—my friend in prison with whom I'd shared a notable foray into eastern mysticism—but not by name. I would just refer to him as a friend in prison. I can't say why, but this time was different. When I got to that part, I blurted Paul's name out. Immediately, Fred interrupted me.

"I'm sorry," he said, "did you say 'Paul Stavenjord'?"

I answered, "Yes."

He said, "I know him. He's my neighbor. Finish your story, and then we will talk."

I quickly finished and asked Fred to tell me more.

"When did you last Google Paul?" he asked.

"I never have."

"Go home and search him out, then we can talk tomorrow. But please don't believe everything you read about him."

That night, I found Paul on the internet. He had become famous for three things. He was an accomplished Native American flute carver and player. He made and sold flutes for up to $2500 each. Next, he was really big into the New Age Movement; Shirley MacLaine was his friend (this came as no surprise to me after all the weird spiritual dabbling we'd done in prison). Finally, he was back in prison serving two consecutive ninety-nine-year terms for a double murder on Memorial Day weekend in 1997. I spent the evening and late into the night reading everything I could find about him.

The next day, Fred told me he knew Paul and both the victims, a married couple. Fred said, "It wasn't at all like the reports say. Paul was having an affair with Deb, and Carl came home and caught them. Carl shot at Paul but hit Deb. Paul shot back in self-defense and killed Carl."

On the way home from the convention that day, I had a conversation with God. I told him, "You bring my best friend back from twenty-five years ago, from thirty-five hundred miles away, with three hundred million people between me and him. What are You doing, God?"

He said, "I want you to go tell him about My Son, Jesus."

I started explaining to God why that was a bad idea. After all, I am an ex-con, and I can't even get into a prison to see people I *don't* know. They certainly aren't going to let me in to see my best friend from prison.

It was somewhat obvious that God wasn't going to lose the argument, so I decided instead to give it a shot, just so I could just say, "I told You so." I searched the internet and found a number for the Alaska prisoner locator. I called and left a message. A lady called me back the next morning.

She said, "Do you mind if I ask why you want to find him?"

"I am a believer," I explained, "and I was his best friend twenty-five years ago when we were in prison together. God told me to go tell him about Jesus."

The lady began to sound a bit choked up.

I asked, "Are you okay?"

She said, "Please excuse me while I get a tissue. My prayer group has been praying for Paul for nearly three years now."

"Why Paul?" I asked.

She said, "Paul was kind of a big deal. The whole manhunt thing and his New Age theology and such. We just started one day and never stopped."

I then told her, "Since I am an ex-con, I don't think they will let me just walk in and do my thing. Is there another way we can skin this cat?"

She said, "I have a friend who works with the chaplain in the facility where Paul is located. I'll give her a call. Give me a few days to see what we can do."

I got a call from the chaplain's assistant the next morning. She, too, asked that I tell her why I wanted to see Paul. I shared again that God had told me to tell him about Jesus. She said she would relay the message to the chaplain.

A couple of hours later, I received a call from Chaplain Michael Ensch. "Don't tell me what you want to do," he said, "I want to hear your testimony."

I shared with him my story of coming to know Jesus.

"How do you want to do this?" he asked.

I thought I would go for the whole enchilada. "I would like to come to the facility and spend three days with Paul. The first day, I want to just do the 'glory days' thing. You know—remember this time? Remember that? Then the second day I want to tell him what I have been doing since I got out. The third day I want to tell him about Jesus."

He said, "I can go see him and ask him to put you on his visitor's list."

I said, "I would prefer you don't. I would rather he not know I am coming until we are face to face. I don't want him to have time to pre-conceive any ideas of why I'm coming."

"Okay," he said, "I can bring you in as a guest speaker. We'll bring Paul to the chaplain's office and lock you and him in for as long as you need. Up to three full days if you want. We can even have the kitchen bring trays in for your lunch and dinner."

As soon as I hung up, I started calling airlines looking to book a flight. United was the only airline that could get me to Palmer, Alaska. However, they were in the midst of a labor dispute, and I couldn't book a flight. I got mad and started yelling at God. "I didn't want to do this, and You made me. Now that I'm ready to go, I can't get there. This sucks, God. Do something."

Just then my phone rang. It was Chaplain Ensch again.

"John, it looks like you can't come to Alaska. Mr. Stavenjord is getting on a plane as we speak. He is being transported to another facility out of state. After he lands we can make plans to do this there. I'll let you know."

A few hours later he called again and said, "Paul is in a private prison in Florence, Arizona, which contracts to house Alaska inmates. Can you get there by this weekend?"

I answered, "As soon as I hang up, I'll book a flight." This was when I once again realized how big my God really is. If I can't get to Alaska, He'll bring Paul to me. After all, Arizona borders Colorado.

The chaplain added, "My assistant wants to go also. So we can meet you there Friday evening. You can go in Friday morning. I am giving instructions to the chaplain there. His name is Chaplain Hackett. Afterward, we will meet you and him at A&M Pizza out on Highway 287."

I asked, "Do we need to get approval from the chaplain there first?"

He answered "Not at all. I am his supervisor. I am the head chaplain for all of Alaska corrections."

CHAPTER FIFTY

STAVENJORD

I arrived at the prison but there was a glitch and I wasn't allowed into the facility. I went back to the motel and just waited until it was time to meet at the pizza place. I arrived first and soon Chaplain Hackett joined me. Then Chaplain Ensch and his assistant arrived.

Ensch said, "Looks like we need to adjust your plans to a two-day thing instead."

I said, "I am flexible. God isn't surprised by this. I will work with whatever time I have."

The next morning I showed up at the prison, but Hackett said he didn't have time to escort me, so he would have me wait in his office until he could get free.

He came in about noon and told me, "Looks like you might not be able to see your friend. He is in the hole. This facility has seven different segregation units. I might be able to give you a few minutes just talking to him through the window of his door. That is, if we can find him."

I spent the next three hours following him around while he handed out Qurans to Muslims throughout the facility. He inquired about Paul at each segregation unit we came to. After we'd been to all seven segregation units, we learned he wasn't in the hole after all. The chaplain located Paul and we went to his cell.

Hackett called out to the guard, "Open cell number 22, please."

As it opened, he said, "Paul Stavenjord. Step out here please. I am Chaplain Hackett."

Paul came out and Hackett said, "This is John Swanger."

Paul said, "Who?"

I answered: "It's Tex."

I could see the light come on in Paul's eyes, and he quickly came over and hugged me. I was wondering if he had activities lined up for the evening, so I asked, "How much time do you have, Paul?"

"Shoot," he replied, "I've got two ninety-nine year sentences. I'm not going anywhere."

I said, "Dude, I wouldn't worry about that second one."

Chaplain Hackett was obviously annoyed at my statement, but Paul laughed. We walked to the chaplain's office and Hackett locked us in and left us there.

I decided to skip the glory days and just cut to the present. "Paul, I talked to your old friend Fred and he said the papers were wrong in their reports. He said Carl shot Deb, then you shot Carl. I just have one question about that. Who shot first?"

He started crying. "I'm really not sure. It's all kind of a blur now."

Then I asked, "Where are you at with God on this whole thing, Paul?"

He answered, "You know I am here for a purpose. Mother Nature causes everything."

I decided it wasn't the time to challenge his tainted theology, so I went back to the glory days. We talked about memories from prison and discussed where we both ended up after. I told him I had spent the last few years feeding the homeless full-time and that I was happily married. He told me about his flutes and his CD of original music.

Too soon, the chaplain came and sent Paul back to his cell. I was dismissed to leave the facility.

The next morning, Sunday, I arrived at the prison and was met by Chaplain Ensch.

He said, "I forgot that I was supposed to host a concert on the prison yard. So, I will be tied up for the day. The best we can do for you, John, is that I can bring out a couple of chairs and place them against the gym wall so you and Paul can talk. However, you will probably only have about twenty minutes before the band starts, and they will get loud real fast. Sorry."

I said, "No worries. God will do what He needs to do to make this happen."

I took my seat and waited for Paul. He came out and sat in the other chair. I said, "Paul, yesterday I joked about you not worrying about your second ninety-nine year sentence."

Paul said, "Not to worry, John. You're my best friend. It's all good. I know you were joking."

"But Paul," I answered, "The truth is that it's your second sentence I want to talk about. You and I both know where you are going to serve your first sentence. My question is, do you know where you are going to serve the second ninety-nine? And beyond?"

He said, "I'm not sure."

I asked if he would be willing to pray with me, and he said he would. We prayed the prayer of salvation, and I gave him my small Bible. Then I asked Ensch if I could give him a copy of *Crucified*, the cassette of my songs.

He said, "No problem."

As the band got rolling and the crowd gathered to about seven hundred, Mike called me to the side. "I had forgotten, since this band of guards is technically a Christian band, I am supposed to deliver a short message at the conclusion. Honestly, I have nothing prepared. Would you want to speak in my place?"

The verse from 2 Timothy came to mind, "Preach the word; be instant in season, out of season" (4:2, KJV). I said, "Yes."

"Are you sure?" Mike asked. "You have something prepared?"

I said, "I try to stay prepared to speak." As I was walking to the podium I began talking to God. I said, "God, you'd better do something. I'm empty. Think of something quick, or we are going to look really bad."

I stepped up to the microphone and looked at the massive crowd that had gathered. I thought, *Open your mouth and God will give you the words.* I said, "I have good news for all you guys. I'm here to bust you all out."

Immediately I thought, *God, couldn't you have thought of something better than that?* As the crowd started cheering, I looked back to see Hackett reaching for his radio. Ensch stopped him. He said, "Wait, this is going to be good."

I pointed at Paul, and said, "I just busted him out, and I can bust you out too. If you walk out of here tomorrow and Jesus isn't in your heart, you are still locked up. But if you accept Jesus into your heart right here, right now, you can be free, even behind these bars."

I then pointed to one of the gun towers and said, "There is a guard in that tower whose job is to keep your body locked up. There is nothing I can do about that. But there is a guard you have placed in your heart that is there to keep Jesus locked out. With a simple prayer, we can fire that jerk right now. You can have an unshackled spirit even though your body is still shackled."

Chaplain Ensch and I, along with a few of the inmates from the prison church, started praying with inmates. In all there were about 25 inmates who gave their lives to Christ.

After that, Paul and I said our goodbyes, and I left. Ensch invited me to join them for dinner at Tom's BBQ, a local favorite in Casa Grande. Dinner was great, but the conversation was even better.

Mike said, "Next week, we're going to open a faith-based pod in the Alaska unit at the prison in Florence, Arizona. It will house only believers. I am putting your friend Paul at the top of the list so he will be one of the first to be housed there."

I felt like I was walking on the clouds. Then Ensch told me Alaska had fourteen holding facilities where inmates stayed until sentencing and transport to out-of-state prisons. He explained, "Alaska still doesn't have its own prison system capable of housing the number of inmates the state detains. I would love it if you could come share your testimony and the gospel throughout the state. Do you think you'd be interested in doing something like that?"

I said, "I would love to, but I run a large homeless ministry and can't afford to be away for that long. Perhaps sometime in the future would be better?"

CHAPTER FIFTY-ONE

······································

WALT

Walt, my stepfather, had kicked me out of my home when I was sixteen. He was the one who taught me to steal cars. He was the one who put me on the path that eventually led to prison. He was also the one who attempted to lure me back into robbing yet another store after I had been released from prison.

Walt hated Christians and often made fun of them—and me—after I accepted Jesus into my life. You might say I had plenty of reasons to hate Walt, but I didn't. What I felt for Walt was closer to pity.

My family in Dallas called to tell me Walt was dying. I thought about how God had forgiven me and how I had long since forgiven Walt. I knew there was more I needed to do. Beyond forgiving, I needed to offer him what God had given me. Salvation.

I took my son, Bo, with me and flew to Dallas. I wanted Bo to see what happens in your heart when someone close to you dies.

We got to Dallas and immediately drove to Mom's house. We walked in to find several aunts, uncles, and cousins there. I asked Mom about my brothers and sisters. "Where are Donnie, Evelyn, David, and Tammy?"

Mom replied, "They are in the bedroom with Walt."

Bo and I walked back to the bedroom. I don't know if the rest all felt I deserved time alone with Walt or if they simply needed a break themselves. But when I entered, they immediately left.

Walt was sitting on the side of the bed. He'd been sitting upright for a week. Mom told me he was afraid that if he lay down, he'd die.

Walt had weighed between three hundred and four hundred and fifty pounds as long as I had known him and had shrunk to a tiny eighty pounds. Cancer had eaten him away. I sat beside him and took his hand in mine.

I said, "Walt, you are dying. Do you know that? Squeeze my hand if you understand."

He squeezed it.

"You know why I am here, don't you?" I asked.

Walt squeezed my hand again.

I said, "No one else is going to offer you what I am here to offer you today. There will never be another chance for you to find the forgiveness and mercy you need other than today. I want to pray for you before it is too late. Would that be okay with you?"

Once again he squeezed my hand. I prayed the prayer of salvation with him and asked God to forgive him of all of the things he had done. I asked God to accept Walt into His family and the kingdom of heaven. When I finished praying, I turned to Walt and said, "Walt, if you agree, squeeze my hand one more time."

Walt reached his other hand over and, with both hands, he squeezed mine for what seemed like forever. Bo and I both teared up. Just then my brothers and sisters came back into the room.

Walt died in his sleep that night. I had the honor of officiating at his memorial service a couple of days later.

Walt had lived the life of a gambler. He had wasted almost everything he ever had either at the tables or by simply banking on a better return from some situations that were impossible. One of his many favorite songs was "The Gambler" by Kenny Rogers. While I had played that song myself many times, I never truly understood one line in it until Walt passed: "*Somewhere in the darkness, the gambler, he broke even.*"

Walt left this poker table we call life with the same thing he entered it with—nothing. I, however, was finally free from the bondage that had plagued me for most of my life: the need to please Walt and the inability to do so.

CHAPTER FIFTY-TWO

ACTS 6:2

The attacks of September 11, 2001, had devastated our country and also bankrupted hundreds of ministries throughout America. Many donors began diverting their giving to national efforts such as the United Way and the Red Cross. Many people also lost fortunes on the stock markets, which resulted in shrinking disposable income. At Cross & Clef, our support base was decimated. It was all we could do to keep the doors opened.

I began to feel like we should close The Tollgate Coffeehouse and just focus back on Morning Manna, the food line. But as is my usual M.O., I had to make sure it was indeed God, and not my fear of the future, telling me to close down.

There was certainly not a shortage of signs from God, but I brushed them off. We began skimping just to cover the building's rent and utilities.

Then one day a friend, Scott, called and asked if I could join him for lunch. He said God had told him to share with me a story from a book he had just read. The author was of Indian descent but born in the United States. He was a Christian, and one day he felt God telling him to move to India. Once there, he began feeding the poor and homeless. He said he wanted to spend the rest of his life winning people to the Lord. Within a few years, he had developed the largest food distribution ministry in the country. Then one day he turned it over to others and walked away.

When asked why, he responded, "All I want to do is evangelize. Yet my days are consumed with gathering food, preparing food, and distributing food. The only thing I have no time to do is talk to people about the Lord."

This whole story touched my heart in a "too close to home" kind of way. I felt he was saying that the ministry got in the way of ministering. And I felt exactly that way. Indeed, my days were filled with schmoozing at stores, churches, and corporations to raise the funds and product to carry the ministry into the next week.

Then I would spent time picking up food, delivering food, preparing food, and serving food. All I really wanted to do was to love on people in a way that brought them into the kingdom of Christ.

The discussion with Scott impacted my life in a way that brought more questions than answers. I was lost.

Driving home from the meeting, I turned on the radio. Jackson Browne was singing a medley he called, "The Load Out, Stay." It was a tribute to his roadies and the audience. It talked about time spent setting up and breaking down, traveling, and hanging in the hotel rooms and back stage. He said the only thing that seems too short is the time we get to play. Then it goes into the old song, "Stay, just a little bit longer. We want to play, just a little bit longer."

By the time the song was over, I was in tears. I had to pull over and get control. When I got home, I opened my Bible, randomly looked down, and read, "It would not be right for us to neglect the ministry of the word of God in order to wait on tables" (Acts 6:2).

Just a year earlier, a college student from Michigan had shared this scripture with me. He was deciding if he should come to Denver to help feed the homeless with us or stay in Grand Lake and accept a promotion to shift lead at a restaurant. He opened the Bible and this verse popped out at him. He came to Denver.

It seemed that the same verse that called him to feed the homeless was, just a year later, calling me to stop.

That evening my son Bo and I went to New Community Christian Church where we were both part of the worship team. As we showed up for rehearsal, Milton Carroll, the worship leader, said, "Before we start, there is something I believe God wants me to share with you all."

The band took seats in a circle and Milton pulled out the book *Ruthless Trust* by Brennan Manning. He opened it to a chapter about John Kavanaugh, the noted and famous ethicist. John went to Calcutta seeking Mother Teresa . . . and more. He had taken a three-month sabbatical so he could figure out what to do with the rest of his life.

He ran into Mother Teresa and asked her to pray for him.

"What do you want me to pray for?" she asked.

"Clarity. Pray that I have clarity."

"No," Mother Teresa answered, "I will not do that." She said, "Clarity is the last thing you are clinging to and must let go of." Kavanaugh responded that she always seemed to have clarity, the very kind of clarity he was looking for. Mother Teresa laughed and said, "I have never had clarity; but what I have, I will pray that you have. I have trust."

As soon as Milton finished, I received my own clarity of sorts. I realized that Clarity says, *I'll go anywhere and do anything. Just give me a contract. Give me the detailed plan.* However, Trust simply says, *I'll go.*

As soon as rehearsal was over, I called Raylene. I said, "Meet me at Paris on the Platte." Paris on the Platte was a coffee roaster / restaurant where punks and every sort of misfit hung out. We loved it and saw it as a big part of our ministry. On the way to meet Raylene, I said to God, "From now on, I'm going to trust You in everything."

Raylene was already there when I arrived. I sat down and ordered coffee. She asked, "What's up?"

I said, "God told me to close The Tollgate and Morning Manna, give our lease on the building over to Scum, and we are to move to Washington."

She said, "Okay."

The next morning, we called the board and said we needed to meet that evening. I was concerned because we had a lady on the board who always played devil's advocate. Everything we wanted to do, she presented an opposition. I told Raylene, "I don't care if we have to fire the entire board; we are going to do this."

Steve was also a member of the board and was somewhat our financial guy. When I called him, he said, "If you can stop by the bank and pick up copies of the records, we can try to find a way to salvage this ministry."

I appreciated his heart, but salvaging wasn't the direction I was going. I got to The Tollgate and was lying on one of the couches trying to get some rest before the meeting when God said to me, "Go buy the book."

I jumped up and drove to the Christian bookstore, bought *Ruthless Trust*, and quickly went back to my couch. With a yellow highlighter in hand, I thumbed through it until I found the section on John Kavanaugh. I colored it yellow, then relaxed. I thought, *I still have about a half hour,* so I kept reading past the story of Kavanaugh. A couple of pages further I read:

> *Ruthless trust is like the pilgrim who leaves what is nailed down, obvious and secure, and walks into the unknown without any rational explanation or reason, other than God told him to.*

I opened my highlighter again and dog-eared the page.

We started the meeting with prayer. I prayed that we would all abandon our plans and adhere to God's. Then I opened the book and read the story about Kavanaugh. I immediately moved on to the quote about the pilgrim. As soon as I finished reading, Ms. Devil's Advocate raised her hand as if she wanted to speak. *Give me my guns, God,* I thought, *and let the firings begin.*

Ms. Advocate said, "I make a motion that we support John and Raylene in whatever they feel God is telling them to do."

Immediately Steve said, "I second that motion."

Before I could think, there was a unanimous vote. I started to cry. God said, "I thought you said you were going to trust Me."

I told Him, "I do. It's people I don't trust."

He said, "Trust me with people."

We told them what God had showed me we were to do, and they were all on board.

The next morning I was thinking about how we were going to tell the new monsignor of the cathedral that we were leaving. When we arrived at his office, he called us in. He said, "We have decided that since the food line is at a Catholic building, it needs to be run and staffed by Catholics. Please consider this as your notice that we will be taking over at the end of the month."

God is so good.

CHAPTER FIFTY-THREE

PILGRIMS

Within a few weeks we were on our way to Washington. We sold our townhouse, packed up everything we could take, and hit the road. We were without a plan other than "Obey God." We loved it.

For two months we stayed in a small cabin near Island Lake that a friend rented to us. This is where we were living when God told me to start seriously writing my first book, *Shackled.* I had plenty of notes and journal material but considered myself anything except a writer. I began anyway. I would get in a few chapters and decide that I was getting better at writing. Then I would back up and rewrite. Over and over. And then do it again. It dragged on and on.

We ended up buying a house in Olalla, a rural town on the peninsula across the Puget Sound from Seattle. We were busy looking for where God wanted us to serve. Someone from church mentioned that several ministries pulled together every Saturday and met under a bridge in Tacoma to feed the homeless. We began going there every week. We handed out socks and hotdogs. We also helped serve chili and sometimes stew.

One of the ministries hired a couple of the homeless to help with security. It wasn't the greatest of ideas. The guys were always quick to take down anyone who wasn't totally in line. They also took more than their share of food and helped their friends move to the front of the line. Most of the people who came to help were great people and had hearts to serve; however, the ones who considered themselves in charge lacked the experience and knowledge to handle such an enormous task.

My biggest frustration was with the security team. I always searched for ways to give Jesus to those who were on the edges. However, the security often took that option out of my hands by getting physical. Soon, we began to see that this wasn't the right ministry for us. Raylene, Bo—who was sixteen at the time—and I ended up leaving because we didn't want the homeless to see us as endorsing the physical violence that the security guards were using.

We started attending a church in Port Orchard, a small town north of Olalla. Pretty soon, Bo and I were part of the worship team. I played guitar and sang, and Bo played both the drums and percussion.

If you search the internet for "most unchurched state," Washington produces about fifty thousand hits, followed by Oregon with about three thousand hits. I thought that with so few attenders, the churches would be outward focused in hopes of drawing people in. What I found, though, was just the opposite. Churches we had tried were more focused on catering to the senior crowd and shunning the younger generations. I really felt that I was spiritually starving.

Then one day Bo and I both received letters from the church where we played on the worship team. The letter criticized our appearance and specifically mentioned Bo's cap. He wore a black baseball cap without anything written on it; he didn't even wear it sideways or backwards. Just a cap. They said caps were no longer allowed. There were several other things that were shunned by the church leadership.

Bo read his letter and came storming out of his room. He said to me, "So we are leaving that church, right?"

I said, "Bo, you are old enough, and you have a car and a driver's license. You need to decide on your own what God wants you to do. Your mom and I will decide what we are going to do. If we decide to stay, you can go."

Bo asked, "What are you and Mom going to do?"

I said, "I am not going to tell you until you decide what you are doing."

The next morning, I found that Bo had left a letter on the table for me to read. It was to the leadership of the church. It was about four pages long, and at first I thought I would have to do some major editing to soften what he was saying because it was obvious he wasn't pleased. He pulled no punches. But after I read it, I decided it didn't need editing; in fact, what it needed was to be read by the entire board of the church, the staff, and the elders.

Basically, Bo said, "If you continue to cater to the old people without welcoming the young into your church, your doors will close once the last senior dies. If you continue rejecting the youth, you are not a church; you are a social club. I don't wear my hat to disrespect anyone. I wear it in hopes that if by chance someone my age walks through the door, he or she might think they could fit in here. It is my hope I can help welcome the younger people to your church."

We made copies and sent them to the leadership of the church. We waited, but three weeks went by without having heard back. I decided to seek a meeting with the pastor.

I located a photo from our time under the bridge serving the homeless. It was a picture of Bo reading from his Bible to three homeless youth. The guy had a mohawk and he was sitting with two girls. All had tattoos and piercings.

I took the photo to the pastor. "Sir," I asked, him, "if my son wins these three to the Lord, can we bring them here to church?"

He answer was short and quick: "Absolutely not."

I said, "Well then, we are done here."

I left and went to meet with the pastor of another church we had attended before.

I asked him, "Is it possible we might bring these kids to church without them becoming ridiculed and shunned? Or worse yet, being placed on a pedestal as the token homeless project of the week?"

He answered, "John, I wish I could tell you yes. However most of these churches up here are run and attended by a bunch of old school, legalistic codgers who are not open to any changes."

I was in tears when I left. I went home and told Raylene that I needed to fly to Denver. I truly felt there was nowhere for us in Washington. We were indeed starving, spiritually.

I wanted to go meet with Mike Sares from Scum of the Earth Church, and Louie Angone, the senior pastor of New Community Christian Church. I considered both my pastors. My plan was to ask them both, even though we were fifteen hundred miles away, if they could still be my pastors and send me their weekly messages so we could be fed.

I had meetings set up with both. However, as I got off the plane, my phone rang. It was Bo. He said, "Dad, I have someone here who wants to talk to you. Her name is Shannon."

He handed her the phone and she said, "I just got kicked out of church."

"Why?" I asked.

She answered, "The pastor told me that I need to go home and take out my labret*. He then said that after it heals, come back and he will decide if I can attend his church."

I asked where she attended church and she told me it was the same church we had just left. I then asked her, "Shannon, how long have you been a believer in Jesus Christ?"

She said, "I'm not yet."

My heart was broken. I thought, *My God, they are kicking out unbelievers.* She gave the phone back to Bo, and I told him to pray the prayer of salvation with her, then tell her she now had a place where she could attend church. That call totally changed the dynamics of both meetings. Instead of looking for spiritual food, I was now looking for help and guidance for starting a church.

I first met with Louie, and after I told him what I needed to do, he offered to help guide me along the path. He also offered a three-thousand-dollar gift to help with the startup expenses.

My meeting with Mike was quite similar, except he had me meet with the leadership of Scum Denver. They questioned me and gave their blessings on our venture. Mike and Scum of the Earth also donated five thousand dollars to the cause.

That evening, I sat in my motel room and mulled over what to name the church. I didn't want to name it Scum of the Earth, because I already felt rejected by the people I knew back in Washington, and I didn't want to draw attention. I also rejected all the yuppie church catchwords like *community, fellowship,* and *chapel.* Every word that sounded like a church immediately felt wrong. Finally, after much thought, I realized that nothing fit except Scum of the Earth Church.

---

* A labret is a form of body piercing. Taken literally, it is any type of adornment that is attached to the lip (labrum). However, the term usually refers to a piercing below the bottom lip, above the chin.

CHAPTER FIFTY-FOUR

S.O.T.E.C. SEATTLE

As soon as I returned in August of 2003, we started having church in our living room. One of the guys who attended helped by making us a couple of nice wooden signs for our driveway that said *Scum of the Earth Church meets here Sunday evenings at 6 pm*. Within a couple of weeks, someone stole one of the signs.

Seattle Pacific University (SPU) offered to let us meet on their campus, but they withdrew the offer as soon as they saw the name of our church. From there, we moved to a Tully's coffee shop.

We were there for a little over a month when the manager said to us, "The customers are complaining about "all the Jesus talk." We subsequently moved across the street to a Starbucks. As soon as we arrived, we knew our stay there wouldn't be long, for the same reasons. We began searching for a permanent home.

We found it in the University District, a storefront on the avenue, right next to a comic book store and across the street from a couple of bars. Perfect. We moved in and began painting and doing some minor alterations. We opened the doors and began inviting in the local college kids and the homeless. Each Tuesday and Thursday evening, we opened for The Tollgate Coffeehouse Seattle. We served a hot meal and had fellowship and coffee along with card games, chess, and dominoes. We opened Sunday for church.

Scum of the Earth Church attracted students from SPU also. It was my vision to have the place fill up with students and homeless. We had free wi-fi and food. What was not to like? I hoped one day to come in and not be able to tell the homeless from the students. I hoped the students would bring a bit of hope to the homeless and that the homeless would foster humility in the students. It didn't take long before the place was filling to capacity.

I had been ordained as a minister of the gospel back in 1993 by the Ministerial Fellowship and the International Church. Then, in 1996, I was ordained as an evangelist by the Ministerial Services of Cross & Clef Ministries. However Mike Sares, the pastor of Scum of the Earth Church in Denver, thought I should be ordained by the same organization that held his ordination, the Alliance for Renewal Churches in Ohio.

I received a packet of forms and questionnaires in the mail. I made my way through a list of reading material, including Grudem's *Systematic Theology*. I studied and wrote my responses, filled out all the questionnaires, and sent them in. Finally, I was contacted by the president of the Alliance. He scheduled a time where he could fly out to Seattle and spend a couple of days with Raylene and me.

We sat on the back deck of our house for hours while I endured an interrogation the FBI would be proud of. A month later, we flew to Denver for the ordination service at Scum of the Earth Denver. I wrote a mission statement for our new church and hung it on the wall:

> Scum of the Earth Seattle
> "We don't compromise the gospel,
> but we focus on the condition of the heart
> and not the appearance of the package."

Raylene and I loved the hungry, hurting, and homeless through The Tollgate Coffeehouse and pastored Scum of the Earth Church Seattle for five and a half years.

Maxine, Raylene's mother, took ill and it became apparent that Raylene needed to go to Denver to help her get some things in order. We knew we would eventually have to move back there, so I began the process of trying to sell our home.

One evening a young man came into Scum while I was speaking from the pulpit. As soon as I saw him, God told me that he was the one I was to give the church to. The young man left before I finished speaking.

I thought I must have missed it. However, the following Tuesday, the man came back in and introduced himself to me. His name was Zach. He asked to speak to me. We sat, and he began talking through a list of questions about what we believed and how we saw things.

I asked him, "Have you ever preached?"

Zach answered, "No."

I said, "Prepare a message. I want you to speak next Sunday."

We had a staff meeting the following week. I introduced Zach to the group, and we added him to the staff. I started shifting the leadership role as much as I could to Zach and would often tell the staff that Zach was in charge. In the meetings, people would look to him for direction. After staff meeting one week, Zach pulled me to the side.

He said, "Will you please stop telling everyone that I am in charge?"

I said, "Yes, if you will stop telling them you are not in charge."

He agreed but the staff still turned to him for leadership. It was as if everyone saw that God had chosen him to replace me. Everyone except Zach.

Within a few weeks, he began to settle in as the new pastor of Scum of the Earth.

Each year, I would travel to Mansfield, Ohio to meet up with Mike Sares at the annual Alliance for Renewal Churches conference. As the conference closed in 2006, Mike and I were heading back to Toledo for our flights home the next morning. As we pulled into the city, we were thinking about how we would spend our final evening there. "John," Mike asked, "doesn't your birth father live in Detroit?"

"Yes," I said. "Why?"

He answered, "You know we are only about an hour from there."

I replied, "But we can't see him. His wife threatened to shoot me if I ever come around again."

Mike asked, "When did she say that?"

I answered, "Last year, when my flight was into Detroit for the conference in Mansfield. I called but she was outright against me seeing him."

Mike said, "Jump back in the car. We are going. If you don't, you'll always regret it. Is there anyone else you could call to try and connect with him?"

I said, "I could try Bernice, my half-sister."

I called Bernice, and she said she would go pick my dad up and meet us at a restaurant called The National Coney Island on Gratiot Avenue in Roseville.

Mike and I got there first and took a booth where we could see the door. It had been about twenty-five years since I had seen my dad, and I doubted I would recognize him. Yet as they walked in it was obvious I was wrong. He looked much older but also looked a lot like my younger brother, David. He also was still wearing his dog tags from the Marine Corps. I remembered that those dog tags were around his neck the last time I saw him, in 1978. We sat and talked for a couple of hours.

Near the end of our time together, my father said, "John, my house is full of junk. My train collection, my cigarette lighters, and many other things of not much value. I am not going to be around much longer. When I go, what of mine would you like to have?"

I answered, "You know, the only thing I could think of would be those dog tags."

He responded, "I would give them to you right here and now except I made a promise to myself when I got out of the Corps a hundred years ago that I would never take them off."

"I can wait," I replied. "And the longer the better."

We said our goodbyes and left. That was the last time I would ever see him, and I have Mike Sares to thank for nudging me to go for it.

October 1, 2008

We were unable to sell our home, but we knew it was time to join Raylene in Denver, so Bo and I packed up and headed to Colorado. Raylene and I found an apartment just north of Denver and we moved her mom, Maxine, in with us. She was very ill, so we decided to do everything in our power to help her live a comfortable life for her remaining days. Unfortunately, that wasn't very long.

Early on the morning of November 1, 2008, Maxine passed away. She had an amazing memorial service as people from all over came to pay their respects. She had done so much for so many that her passing was devastating and left a void in many hearts.

Maxine Helen Jones
November 13, 1939—November 1, 2008

CHAPTER FIFTY-FIVE

GOING BACK TO PRISON

It seemed to me that the most natural thing God would want us to do after Maxine died would be to return to feeding the homeless. So that's what we did. But I have to say, it never flowed like it had in the past. There were struggles with volunteers, supplies, and the people who headed up the churches and ministries we tried to work with. Doors would slam shut just as quickly as they opened. To make a long story short, we never really settled in to feel like we were where God wanted us.

Although I still had a heart to love on the forgotten and the lost, I felt really disappointed that God had kept me in the alleys feeding the homeless for so many years without moving me into prison ministry. I felt like I was born to serve the convicts and those locked away for life. Like me, they had made mistakes in life and chosen the wrong path. God forgave me, I knew He wanted to forgive them, and I wanted to be the one to tell them.

So one day, I asked God why He didn't move the mountains for me to go into prisons. He answered, "If I had put you into prison ministry years ago, you would have been able to speak to a portion of people like you, the convicts. By placing you in the alleys, you got to bring hope to the ex-cons, the bikers, the homeless, the drug addicts, and the alcoholics."

I thanked Him. But I still longed to go back into the prisons and bring Jesus with me. God had given me a taste of it through the Oklahoma State Prison at McAlester, and again by going into the prison in Florence, Arizona, to lead Paul to the Lord. But I wanted more.

One day in 2011, a friend of ours named Debbie Milligan came to help at the food line. I had known Debbie for many years from the church where I worked before.

"John," she said, "you do know that you are a perfect match to do prison ministry, don't you?"

I answered, "I have tried many times, and they don't let me in."

She said, "Would you be willing to give it one more shot?"

I answered without hesitation, "No. Too many rejections. I'm done with trying."

She said, "Would you mind if I take your information and give it a shot?"

I gave her my full name, birthdate, driver's license number, and SS number. Debbie kept coming to the food line a couple of times a week. Then about two months later, she rode up on her Harley. She hopped off and came to the head of the line. Grinning, she asked, "Would you be open to go with us to Sterling State Penitentiary next weekend for a two-day event?" Sterling is Colorado's super max, where most will never be released. It is also home to death row.

"Are you serious?" I said.

She said, "I wouldn't BS you, bud."

That first weekend in Sterling, I played blues harp for Debbie's band and then got to share my testimony. We prayed for several of Colorado's most dangerous inmates.

A couple of weeks later, we were at the correctional facility in Limon, Colorado, to do the same. Over the next year, we were welcomed into several Colorado facilities.

Then Debbie invited me to go to Florida with her band to play on an outdoor stage at Daytona Bike Week, and also to play and speak in several Florida prisons, including the Florida Women's Reception Center in Lowell.

We also went to Sturgis for the annual motorcycle festival where more than half a million bikers show up for a week of partying, drinking, and drugs. Again we played gospel music on an outdoor stage right on Main Street.

One of the guys we worked with in the Colorado prisons was named John Shager. In addition to volunteering, he also was a professional Santa every Christmas in the Denver area. At Christmastime in 2013, he asked me if I would be interested in taking some of his assignments, as there were way too many for him to handle. So I signed on. I bleached out my beard, donned the Father Christmas suit, and started accepting the bookings he sent my way.

There were lots of corporate gigs and a few private parties. But the one I loved the most was at the Rocky Mountain Down Syndrome Association where, as the kids sat in awe on my lap and told Santa how much they loved him, I was able to hold and pray for about one hundred and fifty beautiful little children. With hugs and high fives, they expressed pure joy and pure love. Then the next night I was blessed to be able to server as Santa at the Denver Police Orphans Fund. I loved it.

In between gigs, Raylene and I also showed up unannounced and uninvited to several Starbucks, libraries, and hospitals. We prayed for more babies and, although it didn't involve compensation, we were tickled just to see the kids get so excited.

At Denver Children's Hospital, we had a friend named Amber whose godson, Keagan, was in intensive care. She had asked that we pray for him. We showed up as Santa and both of us prayed for him. We held his hand and tried to bless him as best we could. When others saw us, they asked that we visit their children also. We held and prayed for about two dozen babies that day. Precious.

At a school, we sat on a big chair and posed with children as parents took pictures. There is always that one kid who screams and fights to get away. I thought the mother was embarrassed, so the least I could do was to give her a memorable photo. So as the kid screamed in agony, I joined in and screamed along with him.

After appearing several times as Santa and seeing such delight on the faces of countless children, I am convinced that Jesus does not feel threatened by, nor does He envy, Santa Claus. In fact, I feel He smiles at seeing such pleasure. I believe Jesus and Santa do live in harmony. Santa isn't the end of our faith. He is not where we look for salvation. He doesn't take away from the true meaning of Christmas. He is a gift from

God to the children. Children believe in Santa not as a savior but as a messenger. As Santa, I delivered the message, "Jesus loves you."

I considered playing Santa just another opportunity to share the love of Jesus to children and their parents. Our ministry is so focused on the broken and rejected that playing Santa was a refreshing break.

My birth father's caretaker, Mildred, sent me a small package in the mail. It was my father's dog tags.

CHAPTER FIFTY-SIX

WHISKEY BISCUIT BOYS

Bo and I, along with Bo's wife, Hannah, formed the band The Whiskey Biscuit Boys. We were joined by Bury Rasmussen on bass and Rob Horton on electric guitar. In 2014, we were invited to the Dodge City 300, a biker rally. We played and our band was featured on the front page of the newspaper.

We also traveled once again to Sturgis to hang out with the bikers and find ways to share Jesus with them. We spent the week playing some of my old favorite country rock songs, some of my original songs from my CD *Crucified*, and some other gospel songs.

I traveled several times to Dallas to speak in Texas prisons with my longtime friend Rick Glover. In March of 2015, we put together a tour of the U.S. and Canada. We started by going into five jails and prisons in Colorado, then went to Texas for three prisons, then on to Florida where we played in four more prisons and I shared my testimony. Mark Mason, his family, and his ministry, Life on the Verge, co-ministered with us.

In each location, we gave away copies of my newly released book, *Shackled: Confessions of a Teenage Bank Robber.* We were already seeing how my book affected the inmates who read it. We prayed for salvation with dozens and also baptized many. We witnessed God setting the captives' spirits free even though their bodies were still incarcerated.

We pulled out of Florida with seven days to get to New Brunswick, Canada, where we were scheduled to spend three weeks, and to Nova Scotia, where I would be speaking and sharing my songs in fourteen prisons and jails. Chaplain Brent Bishop had secured approval and clearances in local, provincial, and federal facilities for us.

We took our time heading up the coast, stopping to visit with friends along the path and serve whatever needs we may find there. Then we headed up to Canada to meet up with Chaplain Bishop. However, when we hit the border, we were turned away. They said there was no provision for letting ex-felons into Canada. I told them I had lived in British Columbia for almost five years after I got out of prison and had a permit from the Minister of Immigration to legally be in Canada from 1978 until 1983. They said they couldn't find a record of it and turned us around to head back to Maine.

We went to a truck stop diner where I sat and cried while Raylene tried to console me. After about a half hour, it dawned on me that God wasn't surprised by this turn of events. In fact, He knew it was coming before we even embarked on our journey. It occurred to me that He knew it before He even formed me in my mother's womb. My message on Facebook asked for prayer but my responses were either focused on other ways to get across the border or prayers binding Satan and prayers of opening the doors. I simply wanted to know what God wanted us to do next.

We felt like God was directing us back to Dover, New Hampshire to hang out with our friends Lily and Jesse. On the way, I asked God, "Why would You set up such an elaborate Canadian tour if you already knew they weren't going to let us in?"

He said, "Because I knew that without it you would never have traveled up the East Coast." This got me thinking about all the friends we'd visited along the way north. We'd stopped in South Carolina to hang out with our friends Jake and Jennifer, where we got to pray with and love on their little girl, Lura. We had known Lura since she was a baby, and she held a special place in our hearts.

Next we had stopped in North Carolina to spend time with Paul and Sarah, friends who met and married at Scum of the Earth Denver. We were blessed to be a part of their wedding before they relocated back East.

Then we'd headed up to New Hampshire to meet up with Lily, another friend from Scum Denver. Lily, along with her friend Mia, had often helped us feed the homeless. They'd also met with me a couple of times each month throughout the previous two years for Bible study and mentoring. While we were with them in New Hampshire, Lily had introduced us to her boyfriend, Jesse, We'd spent a couple of days there getting to know Jesse and hanging out with the two of them.

So, we pulled up on front of Lily's house and again they welcomed us. We spent two weeks there just getting to know Jesse and sharing the message of hope in Jesus with him. We found him to be an amazing man who dedicated his time to running his thrift store, but mostly giving things away to the homeless in the neighborhood. Jesse, without knowing it, operated the most giving and loving ministry around.

I told him that once he started realizing it was God in him doing this enormous good, it would really explode and he would be shocked at how great God really is. By the time our two weeks were up, we had prayed for Jesse to totally commit his life to Christ and to try to walk in His steps. We also witnessed his engagement to Lily. We were thrilled.

Bo and his wife, Hannah, had recently moved to Washington, so we decided to travel across the top of the U.S. to go visit them. We pulled into Olalla, Washington, on May 31. Our old neighbor Steve offered to let us park our motorhome on his property for as long as we needed.

CHAPTER FIFTY-SEVEN

A RADICAL REDIRECTION

We got up early on Friday, June 5, 2015, with hopes of going to see Kari, Nicole, and Anna, three girls we knew from Scum Seattle. We straightened the motorhome and, as I was clearing off the table, Raylene was making the bed and straightening the bathroom.

I reached down to the floor and picked up the wastepaper basket to pour it into a trash bag. Halfway through the motion, my arm dropped dead at my side. The basket tumbled across the floor. I knew immediately that I had had a stroke.

I called out to Raylene, "Sugar Ray, I've had a stroke."

She said back, "John, I think you have had a stroke."

I said, "That's what I said."

"I couldn't understand you, Baby," she replied, "Your words were slurred."

She called for Steve, who was just outside heading to his shop on the property. He called 911 and told them I had had a stroke.

Within just a few minutes, the fire department showed up. I was amazed that the Pierce County Fire Department responded because we were in Kitsap County. My left arm was dead, and my voice was severely distorted. My face also was drooping. However, my legs were not affected. I actually walked out of the motorhome and sat down on the gurney.

I have never witnessed someone who was having a stroke, but I knew exactly what was happening. The fireman riding with me in the back of the ambulance told me that usually the stroke patent is confused and unaware of what is going on. He said, "I think it was a miracle that you knew right away, and we were called immediately."

I asked, "Why did Pierce County respond instead of Kitsap?"

"I have no idea," he answered, "but it's a good thing. We are taking you across the Tacoma Narrows Bridge to Tacoma General Hospital, the number one hospital in the Northwest for stroke patents."

Even though I had no control of my left arm, it randomly started reaching up and grabbing at my face and touching my neck. It was weird. I felt like someone else was controlling my hand.

We pulled into the hospital and were met by a team of about eight specialists at the door. They took me in and began a battery of tests. Within fifteen minutes, I had X-rays, CAT scans, and all kinds of blood tests. They gave me the drug tPA, commonly called the miracle clot buster. Immediately I felt I had regained some control of my arm. My hand was curled up in a ball, but I quickly started pulling my fingers out and working on building up my strength. For the rest of the day and the next, I exercised my arm and hand.

My life was no longer in imminent danger, but my speech remained slurred and my arm didn't respond well. Even worse, I'd lost music. My singing voice was gone, and I couldn't play guitar anymore.

I was set up with physical therapy, occupational therapy, and speech therapy appointments. Although they were all helpful, I was disappointed that the speech therapy wouldn't address my inability to sing, only correcting my ability to speak. My occupational therapist, Melanie, said she was setting a goal of helping me to regain my ability to play guitar. She worked time and time again to see me through. I knew that I would probably never be the guitarist I was before the stroke, but I was determined to get as much back as possible. She was without a doubt the best, most compassionate and thorough therapist I had ever known.

My doctors said that I could no longer live at altitude because of a heart condition called Atrial Fibrillation. The severity of my condition was such that the high altitude exacerbated the symptoms. We decided to go to Denver and retrieve our things, and move to Gig Harbor, Washington.

❖   ❖   ❖

In September of 2015, we flew to New Hampshire to attend and officiate the wedding of our friends Lily and Jesse. This was perhaps the most amazing time. Even though my voice wasn't fully returned, I managed to mumble my way through the ceremony. (Jesse has since become one of my dearest friends.)

From there we flew to Denver to load up our things from storage and drive to Washington. We applied to the State of Washington to begin volunteering in prisons. Within a couple of months we were in the Shelton State Prison, and as well Kitsap County Jail. We gained access to the Purdy Women's Prison and the Kitsap Recovery Center where we came alongside people struggling with addiction.

We were able to connect with the speech department at the University of Washington where the director said he would actually develop a program for me and implement techniques they hadn't previously used in order to help me build up my stamina and regain tone and accuracy in my singing voice. We traveled to the university for weekly and bi-weekly sessions. I made progress, and I am thankful for everything they have done for me.

We began attending Harborview Fellowship Church in Gig Harbor. There we met Brenda, a juvenile advocate and minister to the victims of sex trafficking. She invited Raylene and me to join her for a few classes on how to effectively help those affected by the sex trade. (Pierce County, where we live, is a major epicenter for human trafficking.)

We applied for admission and were cleared to volunteer at Remann Hall, the Pierce County juvenile facility. We began going in three days a week to spend time with the boys and girls incarcerated there. The usual protocol was to have women speak to the girls and men speak to the boys. However, with Raylene and me, they allowed us to spend time with both boys and girls as long as we were together and never left the other alone with inmates of the opposite sex.

We also received clearance to enter the Pierce County Jail, where we scheduled time every Tuesday evening for one-on-one ministry. In addition, we started going to Naselle, Washington, to mentor the boys in the state juvenile facility. We continue to serve in these facilities and are currently awaiting our clearance for the two other juvenile prisons in Green Hill and Echo Glen.

While spending time with the kids at Remann Hall, I noticed a boy named Jose Salinas. He was sitting alone at a table in the day room, drawing. I first was impressed with his talent, but then I noticed that he was operating with nothing more than a short pencil without an eraser. He would roll up a small piece of paper and use it to burnish the edges and blend shadows and highlights.

I asked him "How long have you been drawing?"

He answered "Since I was a little kid."

He said he could draw something for me if I had an idea of what I would want. I told him I had an idea for the cover of my next book but was having problems getting anyone to draw it for me.

He asked "Next book? You mean you already have books published?"

I told him about my book *Shackled: Confessions of a Teenage Bank Robber* and he said he'd just finished reading it.

"You're John Swanger?" he asked, surprised.

"Yes," I answered.

He said, "Man your book really spoke to my heart. I want to know what happened after."

I said, "You'll have to read the sequel to find out."

"Where can I get a copy?" he asked.

"I am just finishing up writing it and it will be in print soon," I told him.

I asked if he had other art that he had finished. He showed me his notebook and I have to admit it was impressive. Then I told him about a vision I had for cover art for the sequel; he said he would be honored to draw it for me.

A week later, I returned and he handed me what he had drawn. It was exactly as I had envisioned. While it turned out to be less suitable for the full cover, it was still so impressive that I decided to integrate it into our ministry logo.

I took the drawing and sent it to a cartoonist friend in Denver and he colorized it for me. Then I replaced the center of our logo with it. What a blessing.

CHAPTER FIFTY-EIGHT

DESIRES

"Delight yourself in The Lord and
He will give you the desires of your heart."
Psalm 37:4

It has always annoyed me that the "name it and claim it" crowd has hijacked this verse to feed into that "What's in it for me?" mentality. I know that God wants to bless us and I am in no way against that. However, this verse doesn't speak to giving you whatever you want. It isn't at all about scratching your selfish itch. It speaks to the need to no longer be conformed to the ways of the world, but to being transformed by the renewing of your mind (Romans 12:2). What it means is this*: If* you delight yourself in the Lord, He will begin the process of removing the earthly desires of your mind and replace them with godly desires within your heart. Is speaks of giving you desires, not catering to your fleshly lusts.

I think God started changing my desires long before I was a believer. When I was still in county jail, He began taking me from the fleshly state of regret to the spiritual state of remorse, and from being sorry for how I had ruined my life to being sorry for what I had done to others.

Then, in prison, He showed me that a life lived in trying to please others always leads to a life of failures and self hatred. He showed me that I was worth something and my life was worth living.

When I finally found a relationship with Jesus, He showed me that my desires for drugs and alcohol and sex were just counterfeits for what I really needed, someone I could look up to and learn from, a savior and a mentor. And that savior was Jesus Christ.

He then replaced my need to impress my earthly father with my desire to please my heavenly father. While impressing my earthly father was an unattainable task, my heavenly Father loved me unconditionally. When I fell, He wouldn't scold or belittle me; He simply helped me back up and gently guided my bicycle down the sidewalk until I could finally keep it balanced. Then He shouted with joy as I succeeded.

My desires for self have been replaced by my new desires to see others come to find the same saving grace that God has given me. All I want now is to give away what God has given me, salvation. It is my hope that in reading the accounts of my life you might find your own relationship with Jesus. If you have been moved by the miracles in my life and desire to be a part of something bigger than yourself, if you want to find the purpose of your life, I want to help you. Please find my contact information in this book and write me. And above all, please know that you are worthy of God's love.

James Hughes

John and Raylene

Granny, Maxine, John, and Raylene

John at Cherry Hills Community Church

Bo Colby Christian Swanger

John, *Crucified* Cover Photo

Grace at Morning Manna

Spike and Hound Dog

Tedd and John

Raylene and John at The Tollgate, Denver

The Tollgate, Denver

The Bull, my
1999 Indian
Chief

John with Paul Stavenjord, Florence, Arizona Correctional, 2001

With Paul at the Arizona Correctional, 2002

Bo Swanger,
Ministering under
the Bridge in
Tacoma, Washington

Scum of the Earth, Seattle

Scum Sticker, Seattle

Jack and John Swanger
Detroit, Michigan

Jack Swanger

John and Raylene Swanger

The Whiskey Biscuit Boys at the Sturgis, South Dagota Bike Rally

With the Hell's Angels in Sturgis, South Dakota

John Swanger

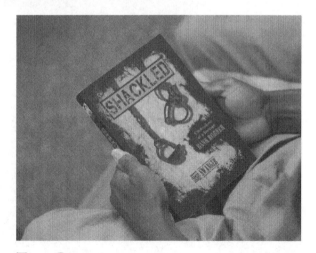

Texas Corrections

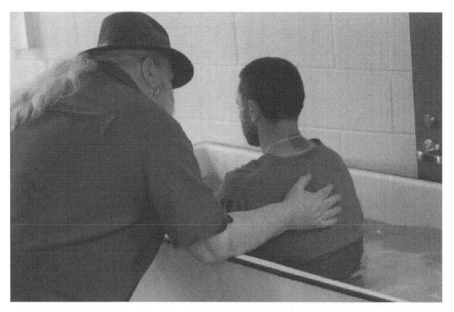

Florida Corrections

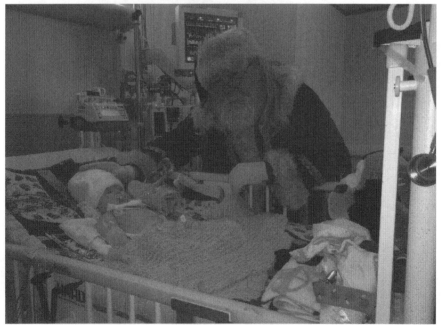

John with Keagan, Denver Children's Hospital

John and Raylene

John with Jesse Letourneau

Officiating at Lily and Jesse's Wedding

Jose Salinas

CHAPTER FIFTY-NINE

CONCLUSION

I was watching an old rerun of *Gunsmoke* the other day. Matt Dillon bought Festus a beer. Festus said, "Much obliged, Marshall." That set me back about forty years. I hadn't heard "much obliged" since back in my grandfather's day.

Obliged . . . what a strange word. It isn't like "thank you," and it's not the same as "I appreciated it." *Obliged* emits a tone of obligation. Sort of like, "I owe you one," or, "I am indebted to you."

This got me thinking about my life and ministry. I am very "thankful" that God has given me many things: a wife, children, and grandchildren. I am equally thankful for all the things God has taken from me.

The fact that I am still breathing makes me "appreciate" our God. I am equally appreciative that, unlike many of the people we have served over the years, Raylene and I have a roof over our heads.

But when I think about the life God has allowed me to have, a life of blessings spent sitting on the curb in an alley sharing a cup of coffee with an ex-con, a broke-down old biker, or a washed-up, homeless veteran who sees hope through Jesus—these have changed my life. Or, getting to buy a burger for the drug addict who is struggling to end it all and sees that I managed to clean up through Jesus. I feel thankful and appreciative, but mostly I feel obliged.

I just want to say, "God, I owe You one."

I see my obligation is to look at the homeless, the bikers, and the prisoners not as a mass but as individuals. I am obligated to look into their eyes and ask God to help me help them. But mostly, I am obliged because I'm not spent yet.

To those of you who have supported, prayed for, and pitched in with our ministry over the years and helped us bring Jesus to those most have forgotten and those who live on the fringes of our society, I just want to say . . .

"Much obliged."
John

ACKNOWLEDGMENTS

A special thank you to the women who raised me:

DOROTHY JEAN RASOR
OCTOBER 30, 1932–JUNE 14, 2007

My mom was beautiful. She was more than a champion. She did more with nothing than most could do with plenty. She took a bunch of kids and was mother, father, and friend where there was no other to be found. She didn't have much to give, but she had love. And that was enough. The shame is in how long it took me to realize that she loved me. But that is on me, not her. God bless my mother. She is missed.

MARY LOVE (TONI) WILLIAMS

My mother's sister was a mother to several of us, growing up. She took us in at times when my mother just didn't have the means to sustain us all. Toni fed, housed, and clothed me. And more than that, she loved me even in the times when I was unlovable. She refused to give up on me, and I am forever grateful for that.

REBECCA ANN HYDER

Ann was my Uncle John's wife. She is beautiful inside and out. She rescued my brother David and me from the horrors of the "Christian" orphan's home we were trapped in as kids. When Uncle John, thinking with his logic, said they didn't have room to take us in, it was Ann who knew in her heart that they couldn't *not* take us. I will love her forever for that. What a beautiful spirit.

MARCELLA (CEIL) HYDER
MARCH 12, 1937–SEPTEMBER 19, 2017

Ceil was my Uncle Bobby's wife. As a young kid, she took me in, and I lived with her, her husband Bobby, and their son, David, first in Houston and then again in San Antonio. Then, at the age of fifteen, when I was anything but civil, she welcomed me into her home once again in Mesquite. Her table was always a place where I could get a meal and some much-needed guidance. I love Ceil, and she is missed.

LAURA (NANNY) WARD HYDER
MAY 5, 1909–OCTOBER 7, 1997

My grandmother Nanny's home was the most like a real home to me. She welcomed me and all my siblings into her home more times than I could count. She always served up a hot meal, and her kitchen table had a place setting for anyone who came through her door. I loved my grandmother and her passing was the hardest on me. Thank you, Nanny, for loving me through the times when I struggled to love myself.

ABOUT THE AUTHOR

Today, John Swanger is a passionate pastor, ministry leader, author, singer, and songwriter. After a youth spent in drug abuse, crime, and incarceration, John underwent a radical transformation of heart and life, which he chronicles in this—his second book—*Unshackled*. Now an authentic example of God's miraculous grace, John has dedicated his life to ministering to inmates and ex-cons, feeding the homeless, and sharing his powerful testimony with audiences across the United States.

John's first book, *Shackled: Confessions of a Teenage Bank Robber* has already been distributed to nearly a thousand prisoners in several states, as well as to inmates in the federal prison system, juvenile detention centers, and drug rehabilitation centers. Countless people have come to the Lord through John's non-profit ministry, Unshackled Spirit, and its mission to share the love and redemptive grace of Jesus Christ.

ALSO BY JOHN SWANGER:

Shackled: Confessions of a Teenage Bank Robbber

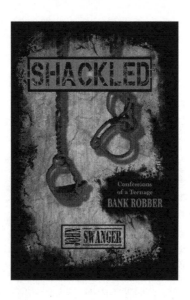

Available through Unshackled Spirit Ministries, www.unshackledspirit.com, and on Amazon.com.

To contact John for speaking engagements or to inquire about bulk order discounts of *Shackled* and *Unshackled*, email:

john@swanger.net

or visit:

www.unshackledspirit.com

All proceeds from the sale of this book go to a fund to send copies for adult and juvenile inmates in prisons and detention centers throughout the United States. The author, **John Swanger**, takes no funds from this account. To date, **Unshackled Spirit Ministries** has given away thousands of copies of both *Shackled: Confessions of a Teenage Bank Robber* and *Unshackled: A Story of Redemption*.

To order additional copies or to make a donation towards the cause, please contact our administration offices at:
john@swanger.net,
or through mail to:

Unshackled Spirit
5114 Point Fosdick Dr., Ste. F-188
Gig Harbor, WA 98335

Unshackled Spirit Ministries and **The Church behind Bars** are sub-ministries of *Cross & Clef Ministries*, a Colorado Non-Profit Organization. All donations are tax deductible.

If you have a family member or friend who is incarcerated, and you wish for them to receive a copy of one or both books, please send us:

Full Name and DOD Number
Name of the Facility
Inmate's Full Mailing Address
We will provide them with copies at no charge.

We hope you enjoyed reading this book
and that it touched you in some way.
We would love to hear from you.